PETER TUDEBODE

Memoirs of the

AMERICAN PHILOSOPHICAL SOCIETY

Held at Philadelphia

For Promoting Useful Knowledge

VOLUME 101

PETER TUDEBODE

Historia de Hierosolymitano

Itinere

Translated with Introduction and Notes by
JOHN HUGH HILL and **LAURITA L. HILL**

Department of History
University of Houston

THE AMERICAN PHILOSOPHICAL SOCIETY
INDEPENDENCE SQUARE • PHILADELPHIA
1974

Library of Congress Catalog Card Number 74-78091
International Standard Book Number 0-87169-101-9
US ISSN 0065-9738

FOREWORD

In the course of our research on the First Crusade we became concerned by the fact that the history of Peter Tudebode titled *Historia de Hierosolymitano itinere* has been overlooked by modern historians because it has been categorized as a plagiarism. Consequently, after the publication of our text and translation of Raymond d'Aguilers' *Historia Francorum qui ceperunt Iherusalem* by L'Académie des Inscriptions et Belles-Lettres and the American Philosophical Society we turned our interest to publishing a text and a translation of the work of Peter Tudebode.

The completion of this work is due largely to the interest of the Institute for Advanced Study at Princeton, which gave us the time and encouragement for such a task. As scholars who have spent their lives *in terram infidelium* we are especially grateful to the Institute and to the libraries of Princeton University and the Princeton Theological Seminary for the most pleasant experience of years of arduous research.

We again acknowledge our indebtedness to the American Philosophical Society, the American Council of Learned Societies, and the University of Houston. Furthermore, the Bibliothèque Nationale of Paris, the British Museum, and the Bibliothèque de Faculté de Médecine of Montpellier were most generous in furnishing us with Tudebode manuscripts and assisting in many ways.

We are particularly indebted to Professor Kenneth Setton of the Institute for Advanced Study. He has encouraged us throughout the years and was particularly gracious and helpful during our visit at the Institute. We also appreciate the comments of Professor Joseph R. Strayer of Princeton University. Lastly, we would be remiss if we did not again thank our good friends, Professor Philippe Wolff of the University of Toulouse, Professor Jean Richard of the University of Dijon, and Professor Hans Mayer of the University of Kiel for their interest in our research. We have in the past recognized our obligations to our American colleagues, but we shall here again recognize our debt to the late Professors Frederic Duncalf and August C. Krey.

J. H. H. and L. L. H.

CONTENTS

ILLUSTRATIONS

PETER TUDEBODE

Introduction

IN PRESENTING this critical translation of the work of Peter
Tudebode, *Historia de Hierosolymitano itinere*, we are following our belief that something new can be learned from the
careful evaluation of texts and that such information has much
to contribute to an old controversy in particular and to crusading
history in general.

Although the relevance of crusading studies to the twentieth
century has been questioned by some critics, the fact remains
that scholars continue to take an active interest in crusading
history; and the First Crusade, by far the most studied of all
crusades, continues to attract attention.[1] Perhaps the paucity of
its sources and the obscurity which still surrounds these Latin
texts give room for new ideas and interpretations, and consequently make research in the field intriguing indeed.

In this search for new ideas and interpretations among the
limited Latin sources for study of the First Crusade, historians
have spent considerable effort in evaluation of the importance
of two of them, the anonymous *Gesta* and the present study, the
history of Peter Tudebode. The problem arose early in the
seventeenth century when John Besly, a native of Poitou, on the
basis of a twelfth-century manuscript given him by the Baron de
la Cressonnière, challenged an earlier account published by
Jacques Bongars in his collection, *Gesta Dei per Francos*.[2]

Bongars's text, placed at the beginning of his collection and
entitled *Gesta Francorum et aliorum Hierosolymitanorum*, has
been called the Anonymous, for lack of a known author, and was
in the opinion of Bongars Italian in style and pro-Bohemond in
content. Bongars gave his sources as two manuscripts, one furnished by the English historian Camden and the other by Paul
Petau. As these manuscripts, if they survive, cannot be identified with any certainty, there has been a tendency to give Bongars's edition a quasi-manuscript status by treating his work
along with later editions based upon known manuscripts. As
Bongars's edition was a product of combined manuscript study,

---

[1] Mayer, 1960.
[2] Peter Tudebode, ed. Besly, 1641.

1

whatever evidence the individual manuscripts had to offer was lost.[3]

Besly's challenge to Bongars's text was based upon *MS Latin 4892*, now of the Bibliothèque Nationale, Paris (our *MS B*). From internal evidence of the manuscript itself, he determined that the author was a priest named Petrus Tudebodus and believed that Sivracensis, referred to by the author, was Sivracum and that the writer was therefore from Poitou. Sivracum is now generally identified with Civray, some fifty-odd kilometers from Poitiers. Besly further believed that the manuscripts used by Bongars had had the name of Tudebode expunged and the contributions of crusaders other than the followers of Bohemond belittled.[4]

Besly's text, along with his contention that Peter Tudebode was the *bona fide* author of the history of the crusade and Bongars's text was derived from Tudebode's, remained unchallenged until the middle of the nineteenth century. In Germany, Heinrich von Sybel asserted in his *Geschichte des ersten Kreuzzuges* that Tudebode plagiarized the works of the anonymous *Gesta* and of Raymond d'Aguilers, who had also written a chronicle of the First Crusade.[5] His arguments in retrospect are weakened by his somewhat irresponsible excursions into national feelings and his lack of access to all of the Tudebode and *Gesta* manuscripts. However, he insisted that the author of the *Gesta* was a knight and that his history was the true text.[6] In France, F. de Saulcy, likewise handicapped by inadequate texts, arrived at Sybel's conclusions by somewhat specious means.[7]

In reply to such charges, Paulin Paris in his introduction to the text, *La Chanson d'Antioche*, spoke of Tudebode's work as having been published three times, once in 1611 by Bongars, who did not find the name of Tudebode in his manuscripts, in 1641 by Besly, who not only found his name and region but the

[3] Bongars, *Gesta*.

[4] Peter Tudebode, ed. Besly, 1641: pp. 773-776. Perhaps the best summary of Tudebode and the *Gesta* may be found in an unpublished thesis. See Duke, 1967.

[5] Heinrich von Sybel, 1881: pp. 22-33.

[6] Heinrich von Sybel, 1881: p. 31. Sybel's eulogy of the author of the *Gesta* as well as his effort to bring Norman nationalism into the discussion is pure nineteenth century romanticism.

[7] Thurot, 1876: p. 67. Thurot has a summary of the nineteenth-century scholarship on the Tudebode and *Gesta* controversy. See F. de Saulcy, 1842: pp. 302-303.

fact that he was a preacher, and again by Dom. Mabillon in 1687. Mabillon's text was a conglomerate and late, but he supported Besly's contention that Tudebode was French, not Italian. Paulin Paris believed that Tudebode's history was in the form of official reports, and so rather impersonal. For enlivening his factual account, he thought that Tudebode drew upon the writings of Richard the Pilgrim.[8]

Likewise Henri Wallon and Adolph Régnier, in editing Tudebode's history for the *Recueil des historiens des croisades,* defended the work of Tudebode, although they took issue with Paulin Paris in his contention that Tudebode's history was a series of official reports. In addition they disagreed with de Saulcy because he had been influenced by the Bongars text and had ignored the text of Duchesne, the publisher of Besly's work.[9]

Thus the problem of the originality of the history of Tudebode remained unsettled after more than two centuries. However, a German scholar, Heinrich Hagenmeyer, in 1890, published a text, *Anonymi gesta Francorum et aliorum Hierosolymitanorum.* The voluminous notes, the persuasive logic, and the scientific method immediately caught the fancy of scholars and threw the weight of opinion against the originality of the history of Tudebode.[10] Despite the fact that Hagenmeyer depended heavily upon Bongars's printed text and that his edition of the *Gesta* has been superseded by that of Bréhier, Tudebode has in general remained labeled as a plagiarist.

Perhaps Bréhier is the most damaging of the twentieth-century scholars to the reputation of Tudebode. He has certainly printed one of the best texts of the *Gesta,* but he has also developed many rather convincing arguments against the originality of the history of Tudebode. He also has had the temerity to rearrange some of the so-called interpolations and place them in an appendix and to ignore the literary implications of these interpolations. It soon becomes obvious that Bréhier worked

8 *La Chanson d'Antioche* 1: pp. xxii-xl.

9 *RHC Occ.* 3: pp. i-x.

10 Hagenmeyer, *Gesta.* For a work in English see Rosalind Hill, 1962. The Latin text, *MS Vatican 572, Gesta Francorum et aliorum Hierosolimitanorum* is included with a few variants. See also Krey, 1958, and *Anonymi Gesta Francorum,* ed. Lees, 1924.

diligently to make the *Gesta* an accurate history by twentieth-century standards.[11]

In general, twentieth-century scholars have accepted Bréhier's views, although some have disagreed with him on the possibility of a joint authorship of the *Gesta,* and others have resorted to a study of syntax to establish the Norman ancestry of the anonymous author.[12] A most original idea concerning the *Gesta* was A. C. Krey's contention that Bohemond used the *Gesta* for Norman propaganda and that the work shows an interpolation which helped the claims of Bohemond.[13]

One important voice was raised against the hue and cry of twentieth-century scholars. Nicolas Iorga noted that there was nothing which prevented Tudebode from being the author of the first anonymous history and that he could have added material later. It was also possible, he held, that the primitive text of Tudebode could have been developed by another clerk. Iorga was not concerned with plagiarism, since he realized it was a popular pastime in the Middle Ages. He was interested in the transmission of the manuscripts and so rather believed that the *Gesta* and the *Historia* came from a common source.[14]

Following generally accepted judgments of the twentieth century, we wrote in the introduction of our translation of the book of Raymond d'Aguilers: "It is no doubt true that he (Tudebode) was present on the journey to Jerusalem, but modern scholars have relegated his work to that of a plagiarism, primarily of the anonymous history, titled the *Gesta,* with borrowings from Raymond d'Aguilers." [15] We then followed the *Gesta* in accordance with twentieth-century criticism.

However, in years of study of the sources of the First Crusade, particularly in manuscript form, we came to the conclusion that a more intensive study should be made of Tudebode, not with the idea of rescuing him from charges of plagiarism, a charge that could be made against almost any medieval author, but with the idea of determining his place in crusading historiography and pointing out in more detail his contributions. In addition,

---

[11] Bréhier, *Gesta.*
[12] Gavigan, 1943.
[13] Krey, 1928.
[14] Iorga, 1928.
[15] Raymond d'Aguilers, p. 4.

our manuscript studies of his work, made necessary by the editing of the Latin text of Raymond d'Aguilers's *Liber,* did not always support critical statements concerning Tudebode's work. Furthermore, as we worked with manuscripts of Raymond, Fulcher, the Anonymous, and Tudebode, we became convinced that they drew upon a common source. This source, we realized, was long lost, and only remained for us as it was reflected in its continuators, of whom Tudebode was one.

In studying Tudebode then as a witness to the common source, we realized that we could not work from printed editions. Both Bongars and Besly tampered with their texts, so far as we can judge from manuscripts that remain to us. On the evidence of Paulin Paris, Mabillon published a composite of several authors; Bongars appeared at times to combine Tudebode and the *Gesta* readings, and some of these readings were incorporated as late as Hagenmeyer's edition of the *Gesta* and in the works of his continuators. The *Recueil* edition of Tudebode used *MS Latin 5135 A,* a manuscript known to Paulin Paris, as a basis for establishing a text with the aid of two other manuscripts, publishing *MS 4892* at the bottom of each page and noting Besly's readings where they differed from this manuscript. The *Gesta* also has a printed tradition based upon editors' seeking to establish the true text. The main exception is the work of Rosalind Hill, who published a Vatican manuscript of the *Gesta* with very few variants.

Thus to sort out texts from editorial opinion became our task, and so we turned to the manuscripts of both works. They are:

TUDEBODE

MS *A,* MS Latin 5135 A, Bibliothèque Nationale, Paris, twelfth century;

MS *B,* MS Latin 4892, Bibliothèque Nationale, Paris, twelfth century;

MS *C,* MS Harley Latin 3904, British Museum, London, twelfth century;

MS *D,* MS Latin 142, Faculté de Médecine de Montpellier, thirteenth century.

GESTA

Vatican 641, MS Reginae Latin, 641, Biblioteca Apostolica Vaticana, Vatican City, twelfth century;

Vatican 572, MS Reginae Latin 572, Biblioteca Apostolica Vaticana, Vatican City, twelfth century;

El Escorial, MS Latin iii D 11, Biblioteca de San Lorenzo de El Escorial, twelfth century;

Madrid, MS Latin 9783, Biblioteca Nacional, Madrid, thirteenth century;

Cambridge, MS Latin 162, Gonville and Caius College, Cambridge, fourteenth century;

Berlin, MS Latin qu 503, Staatsbibliothek, Berlin, thirteenth century.

Study and comparison of these manuscripts left us with the conclusion that the clearing up of problems concerning Tudebode could not be accomplished without textual editing and translation, a double task which we set out to accomplish, the present volume being the translation. We used MS Latin 5135A, the twelfth-century parchment of the Bibliothèque Nationale, Paris, for our translation, noting variants when they occurred. This word-by-word study of Tudebode's history, the careful comparison with manuscripts of the *Gesta,* and our previous work with the *Liber* of Raymond d'Aguilers left us with the conviction we had some accounts best presented in Tudebode, some material quite similar, and information in Tudebode not presented in either Raymond d'Aguilers or the *Gesta.* We further found differences in Tudebode which could not be accounted for by the old theories of who copied whom.

Tudebode we felt presented better or fuller accounts of the judgment at Constantinople,[16] the list of deserters at Antioch,[17] and the preparation of dried skins for consumption during the famine at Antioch occasioned by the siege of Kerbogha.[18] Furthermore, he cast more light upon the 'Arqah question by giving a fuller account of the pact of the emir of Gibellum with the crusaders.[19] In addition, he gave a short description of this

16 We shall refer the reader to the footnotes which in most cases give a more detailed discussion. See chap. II, fns. 52, 54, and 55.

17 See chap. VII, fn. 26.

18 See chap. VIII, fn. 13.

19 See chap. X, fn. 20.

stronghold.[20] Later at Jerusalem, Tudebode wrote the fullest
and most credible report of the procession and its route,[21] as
well as the most plausible account of the activities of Raymond
of Saint-Gilles at the final attack on this city.[22]

On the other hand we found many points of similarity with
Raymond d'Aguilers and the *Gesta*. All three exhibited remark-
able likeness in their wording of the oath which Raymond of
Saint-Gilles took to Alexius.[23] A close study of the reports of
visions in the three histories reveals almost identical word structure in some of the discourse and instructions of the saints.[24]
Although the chronology of the appearance of saints is different,
it becomes obvious that the three writers were using similar
materials—Raymond d'Aguilers magnifying them and the *Gesta*
and Tudebode tailoring them. The three historians unanimously bewailed God's failure to protect his people.[25] They also
resorted to liturgical tags, some of them identical such as the
Congregati Sunt and the doxologies.[26] Over and beyond these
observations, the works as set forth are abundantly ornamented
with liturgical words and phrases. Finally, as we have noted
earlier in brief the pointing of the manuscripts of all three
authors, where the wording is similar, at times coincides.[27]

In the matter of information given neither by Raymond
d'Aguilers nor the *Gesta*, Tudebode cited the presence of Amatus of Bordeaux with Urban as the Pope journeyed through
France.[28] At Antioch he gave the names of those guarding
La Mahomerie,[29] related the martyrdom of Porchet,[30] listed the

[20] See chap. X, fn. 13.
[21] See chap. XI, fn. 15.
[22] See chap. XI, fn. 25.
[23] See chap. II, fn. 54.
[24] See chap. VII, fn. 36.
[25] See chap. V, fn. 5: Raymond d'Aguilers, p. 42.
[26] Doxologies are numerous in the *Gesta* and Tudebode although they vary
somewhat. Raymond d'Aguilers uses doxologies less frequently. In one case he
closely parallels the *Gesta* and Tudebode. See Raymond d'Aguilers, p. 64. *Congregati sunt* is used in reporting the instructions from the saints.
[27] See chap. I, fn. 34, chap. II, fn. 15, *et passim;* Raymond d'Aguilers, p. 11;
Bréhier, *Gesta,* pp. 2, 120 *et passim.* See *Liber,* p. 28, fn. 2; p. 39, fn. 4; p. 42,
fn. 4.
[28] See chap. I, fn. 6.
[29] See chap. V, fns. 15, 16.
[30] See chap. V, fn. 19.

legendary kings of Antioch,[31] noted the presence of Count
Eustace at Saint Peter's Cathedral,[32] and informed us of the role
of Gaston of Béarn in the battle against Kerbogha.[33] Tudebode
also noted the deaths of Arnold and Arvedus Tudebode although he failed to identify them as his brothers.[34] He further
informs us of the illness of Bohemond which caused the Norman to return late for the meeting at All Saints.[35] He has a
rather vivid account of the siege of Ma'arrat-an-Nu'mān and
even reports the number of men in the rolling tower there.[36]
Tudebode also reports the capture of a Saracen spy during the
siege of Jerusalem and the horrible punishment of the man.[37]

As for Tudebode's differing with Raymond d'Aguilers, we
find him giving account of the Provençal losses in Sclavonia,[38]
saying that the Count of Saint-Gilles ordered the attack on
Roussa,[39] and listing the number of men killed and the horses
taken at Rodosto.[40] Significant also is Tudebode's statement that
the Count of Saint-Gilles knew of Bohemond's driving the
count's men from his possessions in Antioch before he set forth
from Ma'arrat-an-Nu'mān.[41]

Likewise Tudebode contradicts the *Gesta* in places, omits
material which some have termed Norman propaganda, and
presents a different editorial tradition. He states that there was
one bishop at Xerigordon in contradiction of the *Gesta's* numerous bishops,[42] and identifies the brother of the Count of Russignolo as a bishop.[43] However, by far the greatest and one of
the most convincing differences between the two authors is their
treatment of Bohemond. The glorification of Bohemond in the
present extant manuscripts of the *Gesta* led August C. Krey, as
previously noted, to suggest an interpolation in the *Gesta* and

---

[31] See chap. IX, fn. 26.
[32] See chap. IX, fn. 20.
[33] See chap. VIII, fn. 33.
[34] See chap. VII, fn. 22. Tudebode implies that Arvedus was his brother, but
he does not make a definite statement to that effect. See chap. IX, fn. 11.
[35] See chap. IX, fn. 17.
[36] See chap. IX, fn. 35.
[37] See chap. XI, fn. 20.
[38] See chap. II, fn. 40.
[39] See chap. II, fn. 45.
[40] See chap. II, fn. 47.
[41] See chap. IX, fn. 47.
[42] See chap. I, fn. 33.
[43] See chap. II, fn. 33.

a hurried re-editing for propaganda purposes. By comparing the history of Tudebode and the present versions of the *Gesta,* we have found further evidence to bolster Krey's argument. Tudebode omits many obvious interpolations and does not make the glaring errors committed by the *Gesta* scribes.[44] Superlatives do not have great significance in the histories of the First Crusade but in general Tudebode uses far fewer in praise of Bohemond than does the *Gesta.*[45] He does not insert the suggestion that Bohemond had some kind of arrangement with Alexius before he came to Constantinople.[46] He likewise does not give examples of Bohemond restraining his troops from pillaging in Greek lands.[47] Tudebode also deemphasizes the spirited speeches of Bohemond to the crusaders and emphasizes the role of councils.[48] He likewise places responsibility for some of the excesses in the Temple of Solomon on the Norman, Tancred, while the *Gesta* makes Bohemond's nephew innocent of such charges.[49]

Perhaps the least studied and yet certainly a most telling difference between the *Gesta* and Tudebode is evidence of different editorial traditions. This difference can best be treated in editing the text of Tudebode's work; however, we have pointed out in footnotes Tudebode's use of *forsenet* in contrast with the *Gesta's* use of *insanus.* We also noted his preference for *civitas* over the *Gesta's urbs,* and his writing of *iaci* (variants *iafi*) for the *Gesta's* Japhie.[50]

We can add to such differences development of what we may call fillers and verb forms. Such differences would come from different recensions of a much abbreviated archetype. Fillers such as *itaque, vero, ergo, igitur,* and others may differ in otherwise similar passages and the *Gesta* may give *transfretaverunt* for Tudebode's *transfretati fuerunt, biberent* for *bibebant, venerunt* for *applicuerunt,* and so on.

Such discrepancies and similarities as we have cited give a partial survey of the problems presented by these narratives and the place of Tudebode's work amid such difficulties. If we are

[44] See above fn. 13; chap. II, fn. 6; chap. IV, fn. 41.
[45] See chap. II, fn. 22.
[46] See chap. II, fn. 37.
[47] *Ibid.*
[48] See chap. IV, fn. 41.
[49] Chap. XI, fn. 28.
[50] Chap. VIII, fn. 2; chap. XI, fn. 10.

not to account for these similarities and differences by elaborate
theories of who copied whom, how can we explain them? We
can explain them by turning to stated and implied evidence of
the authors and the testimony of near contemporaries.

Our studies lead us to conclude that Tudebode, the author or
authors of the *Gesta,* and Raymond d'Aguilers all had unique
passages and different information which make them credible
as eyewitnesses. For this very reason we think that Tudebode
should not be discarded but should have an important place in
the historiography of the crusades. Furthermore, we believe that
the three historians had access to a common source or sources of
information which they used at times to fill in the gaps of their
limited knowledge, and the study of Tudebode further confirms
this contention.

Perhaps the best single bit of evidence pointing to a common
pool of information comes from the account of the Peasants'
Crusade. The author of the *Gesta* was certainly not present, but
he gives a vivid and realistic account of the event, showing that
he was not just a simple Norman knight writing a diary. He had
access to a common source, and Tudebode bolsters such a theory
when he parallels the *Gesta* in places but gives additional information.[51] Raymond d'Aguilers does not go into the lengthy
account of the other two, but his shorter version shows that he
had access to the story.[52] Tudebode frankly states that no one
could see all or know all and Raymond d'Aguilers advises us that
he will not bother with the accounts of other crusaders, although
he does fill in his history with some of their activities which he
must have drawn from some unknown source. As we have noted
before, one of the most convincing bits of evidence pointing to
a common source is the close similarity of the account of the
oath in the three histories, as well as the reporting of miracles.

In addition to the evidence of the authors, we found the
testimony of near contemporaries offered further proof of a
common source. Albert of Aachen, by using materials from
Tudebode, the *Gesta,* and Raymond d'Aguilers, leads us to believe that he may have had access to sources available to the

---

[51] Chap. I, fn. 33; there are many word and construction variants in the
account of the destruction of the Peasants' army. These differences indicate
that the two writers were following a common version and tailoring it to their
ideas.

[52] Raymond d'Aguilers, p. 27.

three.[53] Ekkehard, who participated in the Crusade of 1101, cited the existence of a *libellus* in Jerusalem which was a source of his information. Modern historians have almost *a priori* agreed that Ekkehard had reference to the *Gesta* in its present form.

Closer investigation of this assumption shows, as we have pointed out earlier, a *libellus* need not have been a short book comparable to modern texts of the *Gesta*.[54] Furthermore, Ekkehard's history is similar in many passages to the history of Raymond d'Aguilers and almost identical in word structure with the letter of Daimbert and others to the Pope. However, Ekkehard has information not in Raymond d'Aguilers's *Liber,* Tudebode's history, or in the *Gesta* but which is in Daimbert's letter.[55] In addition, Ekkehard reports the miracle of the marching animals at Ascalon as does Tudebode and Raymond d'Aguilers. It is to be noted that the *Gesta* does not do so.[56] In our opinion the case that Ekkehard had read a little book which is the present *Gesta* is incredible. We have no positive evidence that Raymond d'Aguilers, Tudebode, or the author of the *Gesta* had completed their histories by 1101, and the variant dates given by moderns show the uncertainity surrounding such conjectures. Consequently, since the word structure of the letter of Daimbert and the history of Ekkehard are so close, it seems to us that the two were using a *libellus* (not necessarily a small book) which has been lost.

This *libellus* must have contained factual accounts of the gathering of the army at Constantinople and its expedition through Saracen lands until the battle of Ascalon. It must have been intended for reading aloud and coordinated with the

---

[53] Albert, pp. 394, 471. It is rather hazardous to state that Albert copied Raymond, the *Gesta,* or Tudebode as we know them. Yet his information at times parallels all three of them. Albert includes material from Tudebode which is not in the *Gesta* or the work of Raymond d'Aguilers. He has a few names of Turkish leaders which suggest a common list of kings and leaders. He also has a description of the procession around Jerusalem and the action of the Saracens at the time which is a close parallel of Tudebode. To us it is quite probable that he had access to common information and that Albert added to it with details which he received after the three eyewitness accounts had been written.

[54] *Liber,* p. 23, fn. 1; p. 50, fn. 2; p. 150, fn. 2; p. 153, fn. *r.*

[55] Ekkehard, pp. 135-179; Hagenmeyer, 1901: p. 170.

[56] Ekkehard, pp. 179-181; see chap. XII, fn. 12.

church services to the extent of being cued with antiphons, responses, versicles, and doxologies. It may well have contained pious excursions into the spiritual significance of the expedition. There must have been, in addition, stories and episodes of lively or moral nature which could be borrowed or omitted at will. The whole work would lend itself to additions or omissions at the wish of the continuator, who, of course, would be termed a compiler. This would by no means deny that Tudebode, the author or authors of the *Gesta,* and Raymond d'Aguilers were on the crusade and offered information not in the *libellus.* Few, if any modern historians, have concerned themselves with the fact that not a single eyewitness account represented a person who attended councils of the leaders and knew their plans. Certainly, there must have been a better and more official lost source or sources of the First Crusade. It is incredible that an expedition of the magnitude of the crusade would have been first recorded by a simple Norman knight, an unknown canon, an obscure priest, and a few letter writers without benefit of official scribes from the various households.

That there may have been such a collection is suggested by the evidence of the scribe of the British Museum, London, Latin Add. 8927. He writes *Explicit* at the end of the Fulcher, Walter the Chancellor, Raymond d'Aguilers histories, gives a service for the Feast of Holy Jerusalem and adds: "Lectiones de historia ubi capta fuit Hierusalem Enim sic Incipiuntur." [57]

Thus in this translation and our forthcoming Latin text of Tudebode we think that it is necessary to restudy very carefully the three eyewitness full accounts of the First Crusade with the idea of forgetting the question of plagiarism and with the hope that the three sources may give a richer and fuller understanding of one of the most poorly recorded major events in history.

[57] See *Liber,* p. 159, fn. *p.*

The History of the Jerusalem Journey

By Peter Tudebode, Priest of Civray

I. Pope Urban's Summons and the Peasants' Crusade

IN (1095) [1] the appointed moment approached which the Lord had daily pointed out to the faithful and had particularly emphasized in the Gospel saying: "If any person wishes to come to Me let him surrender thought of self, take up his Cross, and follow Me." [2] Consequently, a wave of religious fervor swept through all of Gaul, so anyone of pure heart [3] and mind who wished to follow Him zealously and to bear His Cross faithfully no longer hesitated but hastened to volunteer to go to the Holy Sepulchre. Subsequently, Pope Urban [4] hurriedly crossed the Alps [5] along with honorable and most reverend bishops, archbishops, and a group of priests as well as highly respected members of the Roman laity. Furthermore he added to his entourage Amatus of Bordeaux, an archbishop and papal legate.[6]

Soon, in the presence of his clergy he began to speak eloquently and to preach [7] with these words: "If any person

---

[1] Manuscript *A*, which is the basis of this translation, errs in placing the speech of Pope Urban II in 1097. Urban's plea was made on November 27, 1095, and we have corrected the date in our translation. The other Tudebode manuscripts do not give a date.

[2] This quotation, Matthew 16:24, occurs in the Missal today as a Gospel in the Common of a Martyr. In the Breviary it is read at the III Nocturn of the Common of a Martyr. We believe that both Raymond and Tudebode knew and used the service books for quotations.

[3] Tudebode was familiar with church Latin and used it frequently. Pure heart (*puroque corde*) occurs in the hymn, *Jam lucis orto sidere* (Ordinary at Prime); *Troper*, p. 126.

[4] Pope Urban II (1088-1099) was Odo de Lagny. He was a Cluniac, Cardinal Bishop of Ostia, and successor to Pope Victor III. See Ruinart, 1881; Krey, 1948; Munro, 1906.

[5] In the effort to establish the Norman authorship of the *Gesta*, scholars have strained to show that *ultra montaneas*, also used by the *Gesta*, is proof that the author was from Italy. However, *ultra*, as used in French chronicles and the legal documents of Southern France, was a general term. Paulin Paris is probably correct in stating that the phrase would be used by Frenchmen as well as Italians. *La Chanson d'Antioche* 1: p. xxxi; Bréhier, *Gesta*, p. ii; *HGL* 5: c. 441, 454.

[6] Amatus of Bordeaux was Archbishop of Bordeaux and a papal legate. The author of the *Gesta* omits him. See *HGL* 5: c. 50; Crégut, 1895.

[7] *Predicare* (to preach) is common in church writing. See *Actus Apostolorum* 10:42.

wishes to save his soul, let him not hesitate to take humbly
the way of the Lord, and if he is short of money, divine com-
passion will take care of the deficit." The Pope also added,
"It is necessary that we suffer greatly for Christ's sake; clearly,
this means misfortune, poverty, persecution, want, illness,
nakedness, hunger, thirst and other tribulations.[8] Christ so
reminded His disciples: 'You must suffer greatly in My name
and be not ashamed to accept Me in the presence of men,[9] for I
shall give you words of wisdom [10] and, finally you shall receive
great rewards.' " [11] When reports of this sermon gradually
spread through all regions and homes of Gaul, the Franks were
so influenced by them that immediately they sewed crosses on
their right shoulders,[12] saying that they were united in one
will in the footsteps of Christ [13] through which they had been
saved from the clutches of hell.[14]

Soon the Franks left their homes and formed two armies.[15]
One part, composed of Peter the Hermit,[16] Duke Godfrey,[17]

[8] The church emphasized the importance of suffering in the life of a
Christian; Epistola ad Romanos 8:35.

[9] Evangelium Secundum Matthæum 10:32; Epistola Beati Petri Apostoli
Prima 4:1. There were various reasons for churchmen combining quotations
or altering them to some degree. They might be discussing a text and using
synonyms. They might be basing their quotation on an antiphon, response,
or versicle, forms that did not parallel precisely the source from which they
were drawn. They might be following a tradition which derived from a
pre-Jerome version of the Bible. Such a practice, rather than suggesting the
writing of a layman, as Rosalind Hill believes, suggests rather the use of
liturgical materials. See for example Hill and Hill, 1960: p. 75 and fn. 7.

[10] Evangelium Secundum Lucam 21:15.

[11] Epistola ad Colossenses 3:24.

[12] Accounts of the preaching of the First Crusade told of participants sew-
ing crosses on the shoulders of their garments. Fulcher of Chartres, ed. Hagenmeyer, 1913: p. 4; ed. Fink, 1969: p. 68. Blaise, p. 472.

[13] Footsteps of Christ. Epistola Beati Petri Apostoli Prima 2:21.

[14] Tartharea designates hell or the empire of Satan.

[15] The Gesta writes of three armies. Tudebode later corrects his own
account.

[16] Peter the Hermit was at one time considered the originator of the First
Crusade. Hagenmeyer corrected this view. See Hagenmeyer, 1879; Duncalf,
1921: pp. 440-453.

[17] Godfrey of Bouillon (ca. 1060-1100), Duke of Lower Lorraine (1089), was
the hero of the chronicler Albert of Aachen. His later reputation was greater
than his accomplishments in the First Crusade. See Andressohn, 1947.

and his brother Baldwin,[18] a shrewd athlete of Christ,[19] under the guidance and protection of God entered Hungary. Then these most able knights and others, whom I do not know, marched along without a unified command on the road to Constantinople which Charlemagne, admirable king of the Franks, had constructed.[20] Peter the Hermit first came to Constantinople on July 30, 1096, along with a great crowd of Germans.[21] There he found crusaders from northern and southern Italy as well as many other groups.[22] The emperor, Alexius Comnenus,[23] gave them a market such as the city could provide and then advised the crusaders: "Do not cross the Bosporus[24] until the major part of the Christian army arrives because you do not have the strength to defeat the Turks in battle."

Ignoring these words the Christians behaved worthlessly, plundering and burning buildings, stealing lead from the roofs of churches, and even selling it to the Greeks. These deeds so

[18] Baldwin was the younger brother of Godfrey and, perhaps, far more accomplished. He established the county of Edessa, first of the crusader states. Later he became king of Jerusalem (1100-1118). Fulcher gives the best account of his work.

[19] The Christian ideal of suffering was expressed in the trials of the athletes of Christ whose agonies were extolled in hymn and homily. Britt, 1936: p. 252, *Athleta Christi nobiles* (18 May at Matins); the later usage of *Athleta Christi* was influenced by Saint Augustine. See Saint Augustine, Sermon 44, "On the Saints," Common of a Martyr, II Nocturn (*extra Tempus Paschale*).

[20] The route followed the Danube, the Morava, and the Maritza. The legend of Charlemagne and his interest in the Holy Land was deep rooted. See Ekkehard; Bréhier, *Gesta*, p. 5, fn. 11; G. Paris, 1880.

[21] Bréhier gives July 30 as the date of Peter's arrival, while Hagenmeyer gives August 1, 1096. Bréhier, *Gesta*, p. 6, fn. 1; *H Chr.* 59. Scribes as well as editors have been confused. Bongars wrote only *Kalendis* thereby dodging the necessity to interpret the three minims preceding; Bongars, *Gesta*, p. 1. Bréhier considered the manuscript readings mixed, with some reading *iii* and some *in.* Tudebode manuscripts are clearer. *MSS CD* abbreviate for *in*, we read *MS A* as *iii*, and *MS B* writes *tercio; iii Kal. Augusti* is, of course, July 30.

[22] Both Tudebode and the *Gesta* speak of *lumbardos* and *langobardos.* Northern and southern Italians were so called. Bréhier prefers and prints *Longobardos* after *MS Vatican 641* (which reads "invenit langobardos et alios plures"). Other *Gesta* manuscripts read "lombardos et longobardos." *MSS BCD* read *longobardos.* Bréhier, *Gesta*, p. 6 and fn. 2.

[23] Alexius Comnenus was an able Byzantine emperor (1081-1118), who was confronted with the masses of crusaders. See Comnena, 1937-1945.

[24] Chroniclers wrote of crossing the Arm of Saint George.

irritated the emperor that he immediately ordered the crusaders to cross the Bosporus. However, following their crossing,
they continued their evil deeds by burning and pillaging houses
and churches. Finally they arrived at Nicomedia,[25] where the
northern and southern Italians along with the Germans broke
from the Franks because of their great haughtiness.[26]

The Italian contingents selected a leader, Rainald, and the
Germans followed suit.[27] Then the crusaders entered Romania [28] and for four days went beyond Nicaea,[29] and upon finding the deserted fortification, Xerigordon,[30] occupied it and
there uncovered an abundance of grain, wine, meat, and other
good things.[31] Upon hearing of the Christians' occupation of
Xerigordon, the Turks immediately besieged it. Before the
gate of Xerigordon there was a well, and at the foot of its ram-
parts there was a spring, nearby which Rainald lay in wait for
the Turks. However, the Turks, arriving on the day of the
Dedication of Saint Michael,[32] spotted the ambush of Rainald
and his men and killed many of them.

[25] Crusaders followed the road along the Sea of Marmara. Today the traveler
ferries across the sea and can see the hilly terrain traversed by the armies. Nicomedia is now Izmit. Peter arrived there August 10, 1096; *H Chr.* 62.

[26] In an effort to show that the author of the *Gesta* was an Italian, scholars
have emphasized the importance of the use of *tumida superbia* (great haughtiness). F. de Saulcy contended that such an expression would not have been
used by a Frenchman to describe the Franks. Paulin Paris, however, noted that
the people of the *Midi* disliked the northern French and that such a remark
would have been common to them. We may also note that *superbia* was generally decried by churchmen as a deadly sin, and almost any misfortune could
be attributed to it. De Saulcy, 1842; Thurot, 1876; *La Chanson d'Antioche* 1:
p. xxxi; *Liber Proverbiorum* 8:13 and 11:2.

[27] The identification of Rainald is in dispute. Hagenmeyer called him a
German, but Bréhier thinks that he erred. Bréhier, *Gesta,* pp. 8, 9, fn. 1;
Hagenmeyer, *Gesta,* p. 116.

[28] Romania refers here to Anatolia. Asia Minor was known to the Turks as
the sultanate of Rūm. The term also refers to the Byzantine empire.

[29] Nicaea was an ancient city dating from 316 B.C. It is located on Lake
Ascanius (now Lake Iznik) in a valley surrounded by lesser mountains. Called
Iznik today, it still retains portions of its walls although little restoration work
has been done. The Selchükids under the leadership of Kilij Arslan governed
the area at the time of the First Crusade.

[30] Xerigordon has not been identified. Tudebode and the *Gesta* wrote that
it was four days' journey from Nicaea. Albert states that it was three miles
from Nicaea; Albert, p. 285.

[31] Xerigordon was occupied September 24, 1096; *H Chr.* 74.

[32] September 29, 1096; *H Chr.* 76.

The remnants of the force who fled to the castle soon found themselves besieged by the enemy and deprived of a water supply. Shortly thereafter they became so thirsty that they bled their horses and donkeys and drank the blood. Others lowered garments into sewers and wrung the liquid into their mouths. Indeed, some urinated in their comrades cupped hands and drank. Unquenchable thirst drove others to dig trenches in the damp soil, and, lying down in them, to cover their chests and bodies with moist dirt.

A bishop [33] and the priests who were present strengthened and preached to the besieged Christians, urging them: "Be at all times strong in the Christian faith,[34] and fear not those who persecute you for Christ says, 'Fear not those who kill the body but cannot kill the soul.' " [35] The cruel siege lasted eight days, only to be broken by the leader of the Germans, who made a deal with the Turks to surrender the garrison.[36] Pretending to march out against the besiegers, he and many of his associates turned apostate and fled to the enemy. The survivors who refused to betray their God received the death penalty. The Turks seized others and divided them as they would sheep, and for the sport shot some as practice targets. They sold and gave away others as if they were animals. They took the remainder to their homes in Corozan,[37] Antioch,[38] Aleppo,[39] or to other dwelling places. These were the first crusaders who happily suffered martyrdom for the name of Jesus Christ.

After this disaster word came to the Turks that Peter the Hermit and Walter the Penniless had occupied Civetot,[40] a castle

[33] Tudebode has one bishop present. The *Gesta* has several.

[34] *Epistola Beati Petri Apostoli Prima* 5:9; *Epistola ad Ephesios* 6:10. See Ordinary at Compline.

[35] *Evangelium Secundum Matthæum* 10:28; Missal, June 28, St. Irenaeus (Gospel).

[36] The siege lasted from September 29 to October 7, 1096; *H Chr.* 76, 79.

[37] Corozan is a vague term used by chroniclers to identify pagan lands to the east. At one time it was considered to be the northern part of Iran.

[38] Antioch was an ancient city well protected by the Orontes River, Mount Silpius, and man made defenses dating from the time of Justinian. The Selchükids had occupied it in 1085. For an excellent study see Glanville Downey, 1961.

[39] Aleppo (Haleb) was situated in the interior of Syria, east of Antioch. It was ruled by an able politician, Ridvan, at the time of the First Crusade.

[40] Walter the Penniless (Sans Avoir, Sensavehor, Sinehabere) was a rather sensible knight who tried to keep control of the unruly masses. He was unable

Road [7] and arrived at the ports of Brindisi, Bari, or Otranto.[8]
Hugh the Great and William, son of the marquis,[9] immediately
sailed from the port of Bari and disembarked at Durazzo.[10] Upon
news of the arrival of these seasoned warriors, the governor of
that city hatched an evil scheme by which he ordered the crusaders seized and closely escorted to the Basileus so that they
could in good faith pledge fealty to him.[11]

Duke Godfrey first came to Constantinople with his huge
army two days before Christmas and pitched camp outside of
the city.[12] There he remained until the wicked Alexius ordered
him to be lodged hospitably within the city. Then properly
housed, the duke each day dispatched without caution his warriors outside the city to forage for hay and other necessities. In
turn, they presumed that they could go to whatever place they
wished with full confidence; but that unjust emperor, Alexius,
quickly set guards of Turcopoles [13] and Pechenegs [14] over the
crusaders and ordered his mercenaries to rush upon and kill the
Latins.

Baldwin, brother of the duke, hearing of the command given
by the treacherous emperor, immediately took great and strong
measures to find the imperials. Finally, he came upon the
mercenaries attacking his men, charged them impetuously,[15] and
with God's help overwhelmed the emperor's men. He seized

[7] The old Roman Road went from Rome to Brindisi and ports of embarkation.
It was a pilgrimage route. See Bédier, 1908-1913: 2: p. 142.

[8] Brindisi, Bari, and Otranto were embarkation ports for the crusaders.

[9] William, son of the marquis, was son of Eude and Emma, sister of Robert
Guiscard. He lost his life at the battle of Dorylaeum.

[10] Durazzo was the old town, Dyrrachium. It was a port of entrance from
Italy and headed the Via Egnatia to Constantinople.

[11] John Comnenus, nephew of Alexius, was governor of Durazzo and was
alerted to watch the crusaders.

[12] Godfrey had left on August 15, 1096, and arrived at Constantinople on
December 23, 1096; *H Chr.* 67, 107. See Nesbitt, 1963: pp. 167-181.

[13] Turcopoles were Byzantine mercenaries used largely as cavalrymen. Raymond d'Aguilers claims that they were either reared by Turks or were the
offspring of a Christian mother and a Turkish father; Raymond d'Aguilers, p. 37.

[14] Pechenegs were used as mercenaries by the Byzantines. They had settled
along the Danube and Don rivers and were also known as Patzinaks.

[15] Baldwin charged the mercenaries impetuously (*toto corde*). This is a church
description. See Missal, Lesson for Ash Wednesday; *Prophetia Joel* 2:12.

forty of the mercenaries, killing some and leading others to his brother.[16]

The sight [17] of this encounter caused Alexius to lose his temper and, as a result, the emperor's wrath moved Godfrey to leave Constantinople and make camp at his former quarters outside the walls.[18] Late in the day the despicable Basileus issued orders to his troops to attack without delay the duke and his crusaders. In the ensuing events the invincible Godfrey with the assistance of the knights of Christ [19] killed seven imperials and chased the remaining ones to the gate [20] of Constantinople. Returning to his camp, Godfrey stayed close to his quarters for five days until he made a treaty with Alexius.[21] The emperor demanded that he cross the Bosporus, and, on his part, promised to furnish a market comparable to that in Constantinople as well as to give alms for the sustenance of the poor.

In the meantime the mighty Bohemond [22] during his investment of Amalfi,[23] known as Pont- Scaphard, heard that a great

---

[16] Forty is a frequent number used in chronicles. It is based on forty days in the wilderness and probably has little significance. In the absence of computerized head counts, the historians leave much to be desired in matters of vital statistics.

[17] Tudebode uses *vidisset* while the *Gesta* has *audisset*. See Bréhier, *Gesta*, p. 16.

[18] Godfrey left the faubourgs of Galata on January 13, 1097; *H Chr.* 110. See Bréhier, *Gesta*, p. 17, fn. 4.

[19] The descriptive term, Knights of Christ, is often used in crusading chronicles and glorifies fighting for Christ. It was more palatable to warriors than the idea of athletes of Christ. The term *invictus* (*invincible*), applied to Godfrey, was frequently used to describe martyrs.

[20] Bréhier identifies the gate as the Gate of Blachernes; Bréhier, *Gesta*, p. 17, fn. 5.

[21] Godfrey remained in his camp from January 13 to January 18, 1097. Godfrey and Alexius made a treaty on January 20, 1097. See Bréhier, *Gesta*, p. 17, fn. 6; *H Chr.* 113.

[22] Bohemond (*ca.* 1050-1111) was the son of Robert Guiscard and Alberada. He and his father had fought the Greeks from 1081-1084 but had failed to carve out a state. His father's patrimony went to a younger half-brother, Roger Borsa. Robert Guiscard had probably planned for Bohemond a Greek kingdom which failed to materialize. The First Crusade offered Bohemond an opportunity to realize his dream. See Yewdale, 1917. John Hugh and Laurita L. Hill have a forthcoming article on Bohemond in the *Encyclopaedia Britannica*. Tudebode does not use as many superlatives in describing Bohemond as does the author of the *Gesta*.

[23] Amalfi was known as Pont-Scaphard. See Hagenmeyer, *Gesta*, p. 149, fn. 3. Bohemond was assisted by his brother and his uncle, Roger of Sicily, in this

number of Franks had come, and he soon learned how they planned to seize the way to the Holy Sepulchre from the hands of the evil pagans and so free it and give full access to all Christians. Consequently, he asked questions pertinent to crusading; namely, the kinds of arms borne by the Franks, what kind of insignia of Christ they wore, even going so far as to inquire concerning the battle cry used in combat. In order of his questions he received the following replies: "Certainly, the Franks always carry the most suitable weapons for conflicts. They wear the sign of the Cross on either the right shoulder or between them.[24] They shout in unison their battle cry: 'God wills it; God wills it; God wills it.' "[25]

Thereupon, moved by the Holy Spirit, Bohemond ordered his most precious cloak be cut into pieces and straightway made into crosses.[26] The majority of the knights enlisted in Bohemond's cause, and, surprisingly, Count Roger was left to carry on the siege almost without a soldier. Reluctantly, Roger returned to Sicily in a state of grief and self-recrimination over the loss of his army. Meanwhile, Bohemond went back to his own domain and seriously applied himself to preparing for the journey to the Holy Sepulchre.

Finally, he crossed the sea with his army along with the most valiant Tancred,[27] son of the marquis, and many other men. Following their passage and arrival in a part of Bulgaria, they

siege. The author of the *Gesta* and Tudebode pretend that Bohemond learned of the crusade from the Franks coming to embark for Durazzo. It is very strange that Bohemond had not heard of the crusade in the months which passed after Urban's call. It seems to us that the author of the *Gesta* and Tudebode were poorly informed on the subject. Bohemond abandoned the siege of Amalfi in September, 1096; *H Chr.* 68.

[24] Bréhier thinks that this report came from an eyewitness. We disagree. It parallels in many ways the scene at Clermont and contains language of the church. See Bréhier, *Gesta,* p. 19, fn. 6.

[25] "God wills it" was the battle cry introduced at Clermont. Variants of it are numerous. Tudebode wrote *Lo vult* and *hoc vult.* The Provençals had a cry, *Tolosa.* At Civetot the battle cry was "Holy Sepulchre." We have found no cry peculiar to the Normans. See *La Chanson d'Antioche* 1: p. 35.

[26] The giving of the cloak of Bohemond was proper in church lore. See *Evangelium Secundum Matthæum* 5:40. For the idea of dividing a garment; see *Liber Psalmorum* 21:19; *Evangelium Secundum Marcum* 15:24.

[27] Tancred was a nephew of Bohemond and the youngest of the important crusading leaders. See Nicholson, 1940.

found an abundance of grain, wine, and other provisions.[28] Afterwards, they marched down into the valley of Andronopolis and made camp while awaiting the landing of all of the army.[29] Departing from Andronopolis, they traveled through rich countryside, from village to village, castle to castle, and town to town, until they came to Castoria.[30] From there they entered Pelagonia in which stood a castle of heretics. We surrounded the structure which had been built beside a lake, and consequently, it soon fell into our hands.[31] Putting it to the torch, they burned the castle along with the community of heretics trapped within. Following these events the crusaders came to the Vardar River, and there Lord Bohemond crossed it with some of his troops.[32] However, the Count of Russignolo and his brother, the bishop, remained.[33]

The army of the detestable emperor, arriving on the scene, assailed the count, his brother, and his men. In the meantime reports of the plight of the count's forces reached the brave knight, Tancred, who immediately returned by diving into the river and swimming across to the trapped Latins. Two thousand of his troops followed his example and swam across the river to join forces. As soon as they found the Turcopoles and Pechenegs

[28] Bohemond and his forces disembarked between Avlona and Durazzo; Bulgaria refers to western Macedonia. Bohemond left Bari in October 1096; H Chr. 91. He remained at Avlona until November 1, 1096; H Chr. 96.

[29] Andronopolis is probably Dropuli some sixty miles southeast of Avlona. The Gesta includes a speech of Bohemond in which he urges the Normans to refrain from pillaging. Tudebode does not report such instructions on the part of Bohemond; Bréhier, Gesta, pp. 20, 22.

[30] Castoria is now called Kastoria. It was an important fortress taken by Robert Guiscard in 1082 and later retaken by Alexius. Bohemond celebrated Christmas at Castoria; H Chr. 108.

[31] Pelagonia was in northwest Macedonia. This was probably the plain of Monastir. The heretics have been variously identified as Manichaean, probably Bogomiles, and Paulicians. See Bréhier, Gesta, p. 23, fn. 6. During this march the author of the Gesta begins to use the first person. One manuscript of Tudebode does so and the others do not. Modern historians place too much emphasis on the first person and think that it means that the writer was present. We think that it reveals the fact that copyists were often careless in the use of first and third person and that the usage of first person has little significance. It seems to point to a common source.

[32] The Vardar River crossed the Via Egnatia. The lower route taken by Bohemond went through high terrain and was extremely difficult. Bréhier thinks that Bohemond crossed north of Topchin. See Bréhier, Gesta, p. 23, fn. 7.

[33] This was Geoffrey, Count of Russignolo. The Gesta writes of the count and his brothers. Tudebode writes of the count and his brother, a bishop. See Bréhier, Gesta, p. 22.

locked in battle with their friends, they charged them courageously and overwhelmed them expertly. They carried many
bound prisoners to Lord Bohemond, that wise Norman, who
addressed them so: "You miserable people, why do you wish to
kill Christians and me? I have no quarrel with your emperor."

To this query the prisoners replied: "Certainly we have no
choice in the matter because we are bound to the orders of the
unholy Alexius, and whatever he commands we must carry
out." [34]   As a result of these words, Bohemond freed them
unharmed. This skirmish took place on the fourth day of the
week, which is the beginning of the fast, namely Ash Wednesday.[35] May the Lord give His benediction in all things throughout eternity. Amen.

The vile Basileus sent one of his highly esteemed officials,
better known officially as a *curopalate*,[36] to conduct our envoys
safely through his lands until we came to Constantinople. When
we approached their towns, the *curopalate* ordered the inhabitants to provide a secure market as they had done for other
groups. The population undoubtedly feared the forces of the
redoubtable Bohemond so much that they permitted no one to
come within their walls.[37]

Finally, we came to the town of Roussa where we encamped.[38]

---

[34] The dialogue has a few words which parallel Raymond d'Aguilers:
Tudebode: *In roga enim prophani imperatoris; Gesta: In roga imperatoris;*
Raymond: *Milites de roga imperatoris.* See Bréhier *Gesta*, p. 24; *Liber*,
p. 40. The role of the centurion suggests the basis for this dialogue. It points
out the helplessness of the professional soldier under command of a superior
The problem is still with us. See *Evangelium Secundum Matthaeum* 8:9; Gospel
for the Third Sunday after Epiphany.

[35] The skirmish took place on February 18, 1097; *H Chr.* 119.

[36] *Curopalate* was supposedly a high official in the court of the emperor.
The term seems to be applied here to a messenger of the Basileus.

[37] Tudebode does not include passages which indicate that Bohemond kept
the Normans and particularly Tancred from attacking a fortification. The
Gesta uses the incident to make Bohemond appear faithful to Alexius;
Bréhier, *Gesta*, p. 26. The procession of inhabitants carrying crosses (*deferentes
in manibus cruces*) was a standard form for church processions.

[38] Roussa was located in Thrace and is the Turkish Keshan. Tudebode fails
to mention that the Normans went to Serres. Rosalind Hill thinks that Roussa
has never been properly identified. Bohemond's army arrived at Roussa on
April 1, 1097; *H Chr.* 127. Bréhier takes the Provençals to task for their later
attack on Roussa and praises the disciplined Norman army. He overlooks
the Norman burning of the heretics' castle as well as depredations acknowledged
in a pact at Serres. It is folly to think of disciplined armies in the First
Crusade. Even Frederick Barbarossa with his disciplined force had his problems
years later. See Bréhier, *Gesta*, p. 28, fn. 1.

Here the learned Bohemond left his men and immediately set forth to Constantinople for conversations with Alexius. Before leaving with a few of his troops Bohemond warned: "Approach towns cautiously because I shall precede you."

When Alexius learned that the most noble Bohemond had arrived, he ordered him to be honorably received and to be lodged outside the city. When Bohemond was happily situated, the emperor invited him to a secret conference.[39]

In the meantime, Raymond, Count of Saint-Gilles, along with Adhémar, Bishop of Le Puy, in passing through Sclavonia, a land in which he should have had no difficulty, actually lost many noble knights and suffered much for the name of Christ and the way to the Holy Sepulchre.[40] From Sclavonia, Raymond arrived at Durrazo, the town of the emperor, with high anticipation of being in Greek lands, since he had endured much from the evil hands of his foes. But soon the wicked race of Greeks attacked and injured Raymond's most seasoned knights of Christ in whatever places they could find them, and they desisted neither by day nor night to waylay them. The duke of Durazzo pledged security to those who entered so happily into his domain. But under the cover of this safety which he had pledged to the Provençals, the Greeks killed an illustrious knight, Pontius Rainaud, and severely wounded his brother.[41]

In the interim, while they harassed Raymond along the way, letters of peace and brotherhood arrived from Alexius with statements going so far as to regard the count with filial affection. While these letters were read aloud, Turks, Pechenegs, Kumans, Slavs, Uzes, and other ferocious people, lay in wait on all sides, hoping to harm the Provençals at the most favorable place.[42]

[39] Details of the trip and reception of Bohemond parallel the story of Raymond of Saint-Gilles. Bohemond met Alexius on April 10, 1097, and was housed at the monastery of St. Cosmas and St. Damian according to Bréhier, *Gesta*, p. 29, fn. 5; Ebersolt, 1921; *H Chr.* 134.

[40] Tudebode seems to summarize the account of Raymond d'Aguilers here. It is interesting to note that Tudebode is more terse than Raymond, omits some of Raymond's diatribes against Alexius, and has some additions as well as omissions.

[41] Tudebode does not mention that the brother of Pontius Rainaud was named Peter. Raymond arrived at Durazzo at the beginning of February, 1097; *H Chr.* 117.

[42] Tudebode adds Slavs and omits Bulgars from Raymond's account. He uses *Athenasi* for *Tanaces*. We translate this as fierce people. See *Liber*, p. 38, fn. 8.

One day when the Bishop of Le Puy had pitched camp, he was seized by some Pechenegs. Without delay, they threw him from his mule, robbed him, and struck him on top of his head. However, since this great churchman was indispensable to God's justice, his life was spared through God's mercy. When the commotion was heard in camp, his companions rushed to him and hurriedly saved him from the Pechenegs.[43]

Soon thereafter, upon arriving at a fort, Bucinat,[44] reports came to Raymond that the Pechenegs lay in ambush in the defiles of a nearby mountain. The count continued with many knights, and after finding the Pechenegs killed some and put the rest to rout. At this time the Basileus sent conciliatory letters, but at the same time his mercenaries kept close watch on the crusaders. Later, they came to a town named Roussa. Here the inhabitants openly committed whatever devilish harm they could devise for the Provençals. When Raymond observed this enmity, he was so furious that he ordered his men to take up arms and to shout his battle cry; whereupon they attacked and surprisingly captured Roussa.[45]

Then the Provençal army journeyed to another town, Rodosto;[46] and following their arrival, the imperials attacked them. In a rear guard action, the count killed thirty of the mercenaries and captured forty horses.[47] Our ambassadors, who had been in Constantinople, came to Rodosto saying that Alexius promised to reimburse carefully all losses of the crusaders after their arrival in Constantinople.[48] They further stated that Duke Godfrey, Bohemond, Count Robert of Flanders, and all the other princes prayed Raymond to leave the main force, and unarmed

[43] Tudebode does not mention that Adhémar was in Pelagonia. Adhémar was attacked in the middle of February, 1097; H Chr. 118.

[44] Bucinat, a castle, has not been identified. This action took place toward the end of February, 1097; H Chr. 124.

[45] Tudebode writes that the Count of Toulouse ordered the attack on Roussa. Raymond d'Aguilers does not do so. We used the Tudebode variants, vidisset rather than our text's vidissent, which does not make sense. Tudebode does not state that the battle cry was Tolosa. The Provençals took Roussa on April 12, 1097; H Chr. 136. See Raymond, d'Aguilers, p. 21.

[46] Rodosto is the Turkish town of Tekirdagh.

[47] Tudebode states that thirty men were killed and forty horses taken. The variants of Tudebode say sixty horses were captured. Surprisingly, Raymond d'Aguilers gives no figures of men killed or horses captured. See Raymond d'Aguilers, pp. 21, 22. This action took place on April 20, 1097; H Chr. 138.

[48] Tudebode states that ambassadors of Alexius would pay for all crusading losses. Raymond d'Aguilers is not so specific. See Raymond d'Aguilers, p. 24.

and accompanied by a few knights to hasten to Constantinople. Since the emperor had taken the Cross, he said he would take the Jerusalem journey as their commander-in-chief and head. After these reports were delivered, Raymond left his army and hastened to Constantinople where he began discussions.[49]

The Basileus informed him that he must pay homage and swear fealty to him as Bohemond and other princes had done. The count replied, "God forbid!" [50] and further stated: "Surely, I shall pledge no lord allegiance on this journey other than the One for whom I have, out of love, come all the way to Constantinople. But, if you go crusading enthusiastically and come with us to Jerusalem, I and all of my men, as well as all I possess through God's mercy, shall voluntarily be in your trust."

While the count was in Constantinople, the army of the emperor arrived secretly and found the forces of Raymond leaderless and so attacked the Provençals forcefully and inflicted as much damage as possible. When Raymond heard that the emperor's army had struck his soldiers, he was saddened and deplored it very much.[51] He immediately summoned Bohemond and the other princes and asked Alexius whether he had invited him to Constantinople for expediting his treachery and had he given personal orders to attack his men.

Alexius, openly admitting the attack, replied: "Yet this was not done by my orders and the damage done to your forces was unknown to me. But this I know full well—your army has inflicted widespread damage to me and has struck castles and towns in my empire. But I shall faithfully make amends, and I give Lord Bohemond to you as my pledge."

When they came to judgment, the count first freed his hostage; after he had released Bohemond, the Provençal army came to Constantinople.[52] Alexius, as we stated above, demanded that Raymond pay homage and fealty to him as the other leaders had done. While the emperor made these demands, the count

---

49 Raymond arrived at Constantinople on April 21, 1097; *H Chr.* 139.

50 *Absit* (God Forbid). See *Epistola Ad Galatas* 3:21.

51 The *Gesta* and Raymond state that Raymond contemplated revenge. Tudebode follows their statements; Bréhier, *Gesta*, p. 32; Raymond d'Aguilers, p. 24.

52 Tudebode's account of the Count coming to judgment is more specific than Raymond's account. Raymond states: *Cogitur comes, preter ius absolvere obsidem; Liber*, p. 42. Tudebode wrote: *Primus absolvit suam fiduciam et cum essent absoluta fiducia. . . .* The Tudebode variants had *fuit* rather than *essent*. Raymond's army arrived at Constantinople on April 27, 1097; *H Chr* 143.

thought of ways to get revenge on the imperial army. However, Duke Godfrey, the Count of Flanders, and other leaders said that it would be unjust for him to fight Christians.[53] Furthermore, Bohemond stated that if the count was unfair to the emperor and refused to swear fealty, he, himself, would side with Alexius. Consequently, after accepting the advice of his men, Raymond swore that he would not, either through himself or through others, take away the emperor's life and possessions. When he was questioned concerning homage, he replied that he would not pay homage because of peril to his rights.[54]

Alexius, who secretly feared Bohemond very much because he had often routed his forces, told that most valiant Norman that if he would freely swear to him, in return he would give him lands equivalent to fifteen days journey in length and eight such days in width from Antioch. In a like manner Alexius swore that, if Bohemond faithfully held to his oath, he, in turn, would not violate his obligations.[55] Then the army of Bohemond came to Constantinople and so completed the arrival of all of the Latins.[56]

[53] The statement that it would be unjust for Raymond to fight Christians follows church language. See Missal: Prefaces to the Canon.

[54] The *Gesta*, Raymond, and Tudebode are very similar on the oath which Raymond of Saint-Gilles took. Since the authors were apparently not present at the meeting of Raymond and Alexius, they must have drawn their information from a common source or else they copied from one of the three. Now the oath is strictly that of southern France, and it makes the author of the *Gesta* suspect if he depended upon Raymond d'Aguilers. It is not very likely that the chroniclers would use the same words unless they had access to a common source. The effort to determine which one copied the other seems to us as a rather futile exercise. See our article, Hill and Hill, 1953: pp. 322-327.

[55] Tudebode omits most of the negotiations between Alexius and Bohemond whereas the *Gesta* includes some passages which Krey has labeled as Norman propaganda. Tudebode omits part of the *Gesta* account which is inconsistent. The *A* text of Tudebode states that the emperor promised lands near Antioch. This follows the *Gesta* version. However the Tudebode variants also state that Alexius promised lands in Romania. They later add this information and use Antioch. The confusion of the copyists reveals that they had difficulty with the secret negotiations of Bohemond and Alexius. The Tudebode variants use language to describe the land grant which is similar to the language of Raymond d'Aguilers: *Boamundus vero fecit ei fiduciam terre sue quod non auferret ei neque consentiret auferri.* See August C. Krey, 1928. The army of Bohemond arrived at Constantinople on April 26, 1097; *H Chr.* 142. Raymond d'Aguilers states that Taticius gave Bohemond three cities, probably Tursol, Mamistra, and Adana. His statement agrees with the Tudebode variants; Raymond d'Aguilers, p. 37.

[56] Tudebode does not include a *Gesta* statement which credits Bohemond with restoring plenty. See Bréhier, *Gesta*, p. 36.

III. The Capture of Nicaea and the March to Antioch

N OW ALL ASSEMBLED and went to the port, where they crossed
the Bosporus and, as a group, journeyed across the land
and came to Nicomedia. There they remained for three days.
Duke Godfrey and the Count of Flanders first laid siege to
Nicaea, which is the capital of all Romania. Following them
came the experienced man, Bohemond, with his army to besiege
Nicaea from north on the sixth day of May and to take up
quarters there.[1] On Ascension Day [2] of the Lord they began to
invest the city on all sides and to build wooden machines and
towers for the purpose of tumbling the walls. Collectively they
struck Nicaea so vigorously and with so much *elan* that they
undermined a wall after two days' effort. However, the barbarous Turks within Nicaea dispatched couriers to those who
came to relieve the attack with news that they could fearlessly
and in complete security approach and enter Nicaea through the
south gate, because no one would block their way or afflict them.

On this day the Count of Saint-Gilles and the Bishop of Le
Puy quickly took up their positions before the gate.[3] Raymond,
advancing under divine protection from the other side of Nicaea
along with his most formidable army, presented a colorful
spectacle of earthly armor. Here he saw the Turks advancing
against us and, so armed on all sides with the sign of the Cross,
he charged their soldiers, overwhelming, routing, and killing
many of them in the melee.

The Turks regrouped and came with the couriers of Nicaea so
happy and boastful of sure victory that they even carried ropes
with which they planned to bind and lead us to Corozan.
Happily marching along, they began a gradual descent from the
mountain top. As many as descended into the valley remained
there, decapitated by the Franks. Bearing these severed heads
within view of Nicaea, the Christians hurled them with sling

---

[1] Godfrey, Tancred, and Robert of Flanders arrived on May 6, 1097; *H Chr.*
147.

[2] The full siege commenced on May 14, 1097; *H Chr.* 150.

[3] Raymond's forces arrived on May 16, 1097; *H Chr.* 152.

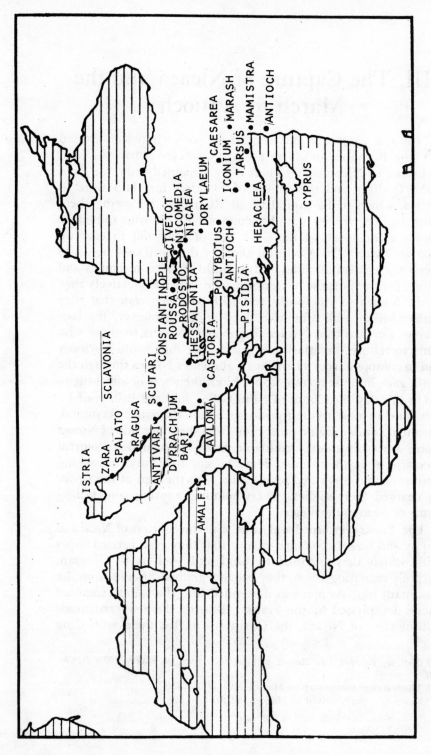

Map 1. The Route of the Normans and Provençals to Antioch.

missiles into the city and struck even more terror into the defenders.

Raymond of Saint-Gilles and Adhémar of Le Puy had discussions on the best way to sap a tower which was in front of their quarters.[4] Consequently, they divided the labor by choosing some men to dig under the tower while the arbalists and archers protected them on all sides. They then excavated to the foundation of the wall, placed posts and timbers there, and finally fired it. However, the job was not completed until late in the evening, and since the tower tumbled during the night, the Christians could not attack the Nicaeans. In the meantime the Turks arose from their beds and repaired the wall so solidly and well that the besiegers were stymied.

The Turks, upon concluding that outside help of their allies was out of question, informed Alexius through a messenger, that they would freely surrender Nicaea on the condition that he permit them to depart unharmed from the city along with their wives, children, and possessions.[5] Then Alexius, dominated by deceptive and unjust thinking, ordered the Nicaeans to depart scot-free and without fear and to be conducted with maximum security to Constantinople.

The crusaders had besieged Nicaea for seven weeks,[6] and many of ours who were faithfully martyred there gladly and joyfully surrendered their fortunate souls to God. Many of the extremely destitute people died of hunger and fortunately gave their lives for the name of Christ, who is blessed and praiseworthy for ever and for ever. Amen.[7]

Following the surrender of Nicaea and the march of its citizens to Constantinople, the emperor was so happy over his possession of the city that he ordered the distribution of many

[4] Raymond d'Aguilers states that the sapping of the tower took place five weeks after the start of the siege. See Raymond d'Aguilers, p. 26. Hagenmeyer dates the event, June 10, 1097; H Chr. 156.

[5] Tudebode omits details of the arrival of Stephen of Blois and the launching of the boats on Lake Ascanius.

[6] Tudebode states that the siege lasted seven weeks; the Gesta has it lasting seven weeks and three days. See, Bréhier, Gesta, p. 42. The city surrendered June 19, 1097; H Chr. 160.

[7] Pro Christi nomine, Response, third Nocturn (Common of a Martyr); benedictus . . . et laudabilis . . . in saecula, Canticle of the Three Boys (Psalter, Sunday at Lauds).

alms to the poor.[8] After our departure from Nicaea, we arrived on the first day at a bridge where we encamped two days.[9] On the third day before sunrise our troops arose, but darkness prevented them from holding one path; and so in separate divisions they marched for two days. In one company was the able Bohemond, Robert of Normandy, the valiant Tancred, and many others. In the other group was Raymond of Saint-Gilles, Duke Godfrey, the Bishop of Le Puy, Hugh the Great, the Count of Flanders, and numerous others.

On the third day the Turks violently attacked Bohemond and his contingent.[10] As soon as the Turks, those enemies of Christians and of God, saw us they began howling, chattering, screaming, and crying out diabolical words in a strange language with which I am unacquainted. Thereupon the courageous man, Bohemond, seeing large numbers of Turks howling and yelling with demoniacal voices, immediately commanded all knights to dismount and to prepare camp for battle. Following these arrangements, he again addressed all of the knights: "My lords and most valorous Christian soldiers! It is obvious that we are surrounded and are confronted with a difficult battle. Therefore, the entire force of knights shall advance courageously against the enemy while the footmen prepare defenses skillfully and hastily."

Soon after these preparations the entire Turkish horde encircled us, skirmishing, hurling missiles, piercing with darts, and shooting arrows from every direction at incredible distances. Although we had no hope of resisting them or of bearing the pressure of such a superior force, yet we persevered steadfastly there with unanimity. The women who accompanied us assisted our forces greatly on this day by bringing drinking

---

8 Raymond d'Aguilers claims that Alexius was not generous. This evidence is not borne out by the other chroniclers. See Raymond d'Aguilers, pp. 26, 27.

9 The armies began leaving Nicaea on June 26 to June 28. According to Runciman, they crossed the Blue River, and at the village of Leucae the armies divided. See *H Chr.* 164, 166.

10 This was the battle of Dorylaeum near the modern town, Eskishehir. The site of the battle is a matter of conjecture. See Runciman, 1951; p. 186 and fn. 1, for a discussion. The battle took place on July 1, 1097; see *H Chr.* 169. The Turks were led by Kilij Arslan, son of Sulaimān. He was called Ibn-Sulaimān and to the crusaders was Solomon. Bréhier surmises that the unintelligible words were "Allah akbar." See Bréhier, *Gesta*, p. 45, fn. 5.

water to the warriors and at all times bravely shouting encouragement to those who fought and defended them.

Then the valiant man, Bohemond, at once sent word to the other division of crusaders; namely, the distinguished Count of Saint-Gilles, the glorious Duke Godfrey,[11] Hugh the Great, the most honorable Bishop of Le Puy, and all of the other skilled knights that they lose no time in rushing to the battle scene. He further stated, "If any man wishes to fight, now is the time for him to prove his courage." However, the leaders completely rejected the request and even mocked the couriers saying, "This is a complete lie." At this time we did not believe the message because we thought that the Turks were too wise to commit themselves to open battle with us.[12]

But the spirited and brave Duke Godfrey, along with Hugh the Great and his army, led the relief forces to Dorylaeum. Adhémar followed with his army, and the most courageous Raymond of Saint-Gilles joined the battle with his huge force. Then our men were astonished at the source of such a host of Turks, Arabs, Saracens, and others with whom I am unfamiliar. Indeed, all the mountains, hills, valleys, and plains within and without swarmed with this damnable breed. Secretly word was passed along, praising, counseling, and urging: "Be united in the faith of Christ and fortified by the victory of the banner of the Sacred Cross because on this day, God willing, you will receive great wealth."[13]

The Christians immediately formed battle ranks. The wise man, Bohemond, Robert of Normandy, the courageous Tan-

---

11 The adjective, *inclitus,* used to describe Godfrey and other leaders, is a word used in church service. See *Inclitus martyr, Troper,* p. 214.

12 With the exception of the Bongars' *Gesta,* the other texts of the *Gesta* do not include the hesitation of the leaders when they received Bohemond's message. Tudebode includes it. Bréhier thinks that it is an interpolation. It seems that Bréhier and others are committed to the idea of the purity of a text and that all else is extraneous. It is quite possible that these so-called interpolations could have been current stories or tags of chansons added to crusading tales to enliven them. This tag reflects a literary pattern of chansons. It was correct for the hero to refuse aid, and it was also proper to scorn the enemy. Roland scorned aid. See Bréhier, *Gesta,* p. 47, fn. 2.

13 See *Epistola Beati Petri Apostoli Prima* 5:8-9 and Ordinary at Compline. For the banner of the Sacred Cross, see Missal Sept 14 (Secret).

cred, the most honorable knight, Robert of Ansa,[14] and the celebrated Richard of the Principate[15] all occupied the left wing of the battle formation. Adhémar, sweeping down from another mountain, surrounded the startled Turks. The most sagacious Raymond of Saint-Gilles, the most honorable Duke Godfrey, the very brave Count of Flanders, Hugh the Great, and many others unknown to me, took their positions on the right. Upon the approach of our knights, the Turks, Arabs, Saracens, Agulans, and all the barbarous breed at once turned tail and fled pell-mell through the mountain passes and open plains. The Turks, Saracens, Publicans, Persians, Agulans, and other pagans numbered three hundred and sixty thousand, and only God knows the number of Arabs there.[16]

The fugitives were not allowed to remain long at their camp, where they had fled precipitately. Thereafter, they again broke and ran, whereupon we chased and killed them all day long and finally seized many spoils, including gold, silver, horses, asses, camels, sheep, cattle, and many other things not accounted for by us. However, if the Lord had not been present with us in battle and hurriedly dispatched a second force to Bohemond's rescue, none of our men would have escaped harm because the fight lasted from third to the ninth hour. But the kind and compassionate Almighty God [17] by hastening aid to us saved his knights from death or capture by the enemy. Godfrey of Monte Scaglioso and William, son of the marquis and brother of Tancred, both distinguished knights, lost their lives along with other knights and footmen whose names I do not know.[18]

[14] Robert of Ansa was probably from Ansa, which was close to Potenza in southern Italy. See Hagenmeyer, *Gesta*, p. 154; *Honestum* was a church word. See Common of One Martyr (Response, Second Nocturn, *extra Tempus Paschale*).

[15] Richard of the Principate of Salerno was a cousin of Bohemond and nephew of Robert Guiscard. His father was named William. See Bréhier, *Gesta*, p. 13, fn. 8.

[16] The Agulans have never been satisfactorily identified. Paulin Paris thinks that they were from Fez in Africa. *See La Chanson d'Antioche*, 2, p. 305, also Hagenmeyer, *Gesta*, p. 314, fn. 14, and Bréhier, *Gesta*, p. 48, fn. 2. The number of three hundred and sixty thousand is incredible. Fulcher follows the *Gesta*. Raymond d'Aguilers, who was not reluctant to exaggerate, gave only one hundred and fifty thousand. See *Liber*, p. 45.

[17] The words *omnipotens pius* and *misericors* are terms used in prayers to God.

[18] Godfrey of Monte Scaglioso in the diocese of Matera was perhaps mentioned as Hunfredus earlier in the *Gesta*. See Bréhier, *Gesta*, p. 21, fn. 5. William was Tancred's brother.

How could any man ever be so wise and erudite as to have the temerity to discourse on the skill, courage, and strength of the Turks, who thought that they could terrify the Frankish army with threats of arrows as they had terrorized the Arabs, Saracens, Armenians, Syrians, and Greeks. But, God willing, may they never be as strong as our men in appearance, deed, or ideas. However, they claim to be of Frankish descent, and in the nature of things only the Franks and themselves are knights.[19] None can deny that I speak truthfully in the following statement: [20] "Certainly, if they had stood steadfast in the faith of Christ and Christianity and believed in the creed and faith; namely, one God being triune, born of a virgin mother, crucified, resurrected, and finally had they acknowledged the sending of the perfect Holy Spirit as an aid, and recognized thereafter His equally reigning in heaven and earth; if, I say, they had so believed in right spirit and faith, no one could have found more skilled, courageous, and clever warriors than those Turks." [21] The battle at Dorylaeum was fought on the first day of July.[22]

The foes of God and sacred Christianity fled helter-skelter for four days and nights after their defeat. It so happened that the Turkish leader, Kilij Arslan, son of the old Sulaiman,[23] in his flight from Nicaea one day met ten thousand Arabs who posed this question: "Oh! unhappy and most wretched of all pagans, why do you flee this far in terror?" [24]

Kilij Arslan sadly replied: "Despite the fact that I had whipped all of the Franks and thought at that time to have them in captivity; indeed in a short time I hoped to have them bound together when, lo and behold, I looked back and saw such a swarm of Franks that if you or anyone else had been there you would have thought that all the mountains, hills, valleys, and all spots were covered with the great horde. Upon sight of them,

---

[19] Bréhier thinks that there was a legend which made Turks and Franks descended from Trojans. See Bréhier, *Gesta*, p. 51, fn. 4; Rabanus Maurus, *De Universo*, pp. 439-440.

[20] This passage is the work of a cleric. He uses parts of the *Credo* along with tags, *Unum Deum in Trinitate, fidei Christianae*, to carry along his story.

[21] The word *consolatione* used in connection with the Holy Spirit means aid or encouragement. *Mente* is not restricted to the mind. See Blaise, pp. 159, 183.

[22] See *H Chr.* 169.

[23] The chroniclers called Kilij Arslan *Solimanus Dux*.

[24] *Gentilium* usually refers to pagan people in church Latin. A cleric would think that the Turks would address themselves as pagans.

we suddenly fled and were so terror stricken that we scarcely evaded the Franks, and so this explains why we are in a state of hysteria here. If you believe me and my story, depart from this place because if the Franks can only discover your army, hardly any one of you will survive." [25] The Arabs, upon hearing this report, beat a hasty retreat and scattered throughout Romania.

Then we followed in hot pursuit of those most wicked Turks, who were daily fleeing before us. When they arrived at castles or towns, the Turks tricked and deceived the inhabitants with the following words: "We have overcome all Christians and subdued them incessantly so that already none of them will ever have the nerve to rise against us, so permit us to enter." Gaining entrance they pillaged churches, homes, and everything else, and stole horses, asses, mules, gold, silver, and whatever else they could find. In addition, the Turks carried away Christian children and used a scorched earth policy as they fled terror stricken before our vanguard.

We, in turn, scarcely escaped death while pursuing the enemy through dry, uninhabitable wastelands, where hunger and thirst beset us at every turn.[26] Our only food consisted of spiney plants picked at random and rubbed off by hand, and so on such fare we eked out an existence. Many of our knights took to foot because most of the horses died in the desert.[27] The scarcity of horses caused us to substitute oxen for battle steeds, and we were in such dire straits that goats, sheep, and dogs were used as pack animals.

Gradually we entered a lush land filled with essential foods as well as delicacies and all kinds of provisions. At last we arrived at Iconium, where the natives of this land advised and urged us to carry full bottles of water because the countryside

[25] We have another digression from straight history. Some of the language in this speech, *omnes montes et colles et valles* repeats descriptive terms used for the battle of Dorylaeum.

[26] The route between Dorylaeum and Iconium is conjectural. Bréhier thinks that the crusaders traversed the desert plateau of Lycaonia in July when the heat was intense. See Bréhier, *Gesta,* p. 55, fn. 3. The description of the desert is in the language of the homilies and follows in part *Liber Psalmorum* 62:3; *Epistola ad Corinthios Secunda.* 11:27

[27] Tudebode and several *Gesta* manuscripts err in using *equitum* rather than *equorum.* See Bréhier, *Gesta,* p. 54, for variants.

for one day's journey was very arid.[28] Following their advice, we came to a river where we spent two days. Our scouts then reconnoitered until they came to Heraclea, where a large number of Turks awaited and watched for the favorable moment to harm and sadden the soldiers of Christ.[29] The knights of Almighty God, upon discovery of the Turks, courageously charged them. The Turkish force, broken by God's nod on this day, fled in wild disorder as swiftly as an arrow zooms from the bowstring of an experienced archer. After this encounter our army immediately occupied the city and remained there for four days.

Here the honorable and high spirited knight, Tancred, son of the marquis, and distinguished Count Baldwin, brother of Duke Godfrey, left the main army and marched into the valley of Botrenthrot.[30] In turn, Tancred, along with his knights, broke away from Baldwin's force and approached Tarsus, where the Turkish inhabitants swarmed out *en masse* against him, prepared to battle with the Christians.[31] In response, our army by advancing and fighting them, caused their foes to beat a hasty retreat to Tarsus. Tancred, wise man and honorable Christian knight, followed in hot pursuit and then pitched camp in front of the city. The wise and famous man, Count Baldwin, approaching from another direction with his army, requested and prayed the high-spirited Tancred that in the intent of a most amicable friendship he consider receiving him as a co-partner in Tarsus.[32] The handsome Tancred replied. "I shall have nothing to do with such an accord."

In the meantime the frightened Turks fled at nightfall, and the remaining citizens of Tarsus under the cover of night came

28 Iconium (Konya) was deserted when the crusaders arrived around the middle of August, 1097; *H Chr.* 178.

29 Heraclea (Ereghli) was defended by troops of the Dānishmendids and Hasan of Cappadocia, who fled when the crusaders approached. The Christians remained in Heraclea from September 10 to September 13, 1097; *H Chr.* 181, 183.

30 The location of Botrenthrot is undetermined. See Hagenmeyer, *Gesta*, p. 217, fn. 42.

31 Tarsus was an important city in Cilicia and was the birthplace of Paul. It was largely inhabitated by Greeks and Armenians. See Nicholson, 1940, for a summary of the Baldwin and Tancred quarrel. Tancred and Baldwin separated from the army on September 14, 1097, and arrived before Tarsus on September 21, 1097. See *H Chr.* 182, 184.

32 See Radulphus Cadomensis, *Gesta Tancredi*, p. 633, for details on the controversy.

from the city screaming and yelling in a loud voice, "Hurry, invincible Franks, hurry into Tarsus; the scared Turks have fled." Then as night faded into dawn the leaders of Tarsus came and voluntarily surrendered it, saying to the quarreling Baldwin and Tancred: "Stop it, lords; stop it. We entreat and request that the man who yesterday fought so courageously against the Turks shall be our lord and ruler."

The able Count Baldwin, continuing to bicker and wrangle, proposed to the most experienced Tancred, "Let's enter Tarsus together, plunder it, and let the booty and loot go to the strong."

In reply the most courageous Tancred said, "Count me out. I shall not rob the Christian men of this city who have chosen me as their lord and who wish me to remain." But the brave man, Tancred, finally capitulated to the very wise Count Baldwin because of the superiority of his army and thereafter begrudgingly withdrew from Tarsus and courageously marched away with his men. Two very excellent cities, Adana and Mamistra, along with many castles, placed themselves under the rule of Tancred.[33]

The chief body of crusaders, composed of Raymond, Count of Saint-Gilles, the most learned Bohemond, Duke Godfrey, and other leaders, entered Armenian land, inflamed and thirsting for Turkish blood.[34] Finally they came to an impregnable castle which thwarted them. There was a native of the area named Simeon, who sought the fort so that he could defend it [35] from falling into Turkish hands. Consequently, they gave him possession, and he dwelled there with his people. Departing this place we arrived at Caesarea of Cappadocia after a pleasant journey.[36] Leaving Cappadocia we came to a most beautiful and rich city which the Turks had invested for three weeks but had failed to capture before our arrival. Upon our advent, the

[33] Adana was a Cilician city at the foot of the Taurus mountains and east of Tarsus. Mamistra (Misis) was also a Cilician city east of Adana and on the right bank of the river Djihoun.

[34] The Christians who were thirsting for blood (*sitientes atque estuantes*) are described in words of the church service. See Blaise, pp. 160, 556.

[35] Little Armenia was largely inhabited by Armenians. See Hagenmeyer, *Gesta*, p. 227, fn. 6, for a discussion of Simeon. The crusaders arrived at the fort on September 25, 1097; *H Chr*. 185.

[36] Caesarea (Kayseri) was in Cappadocia, a region of central Anatolia. The crusaders entered here at the end of September, probably September 27, 1097; *H Chr*. 186.

natives happily turned the place over to us.[37] A petty knight,
Peter of Aulps,[38] anxious to secure possession of the city from
all of the lords, promised to defend it in fealty to God, the
Holy Sepulchre, the crusading lords, and Alexius. In a bene-
ficient spirit they granted it to him freely.[39]

At sundown Bohemond heard that a large group of Turks
who had besieged the city were in our vicinity. Immediately,
accompanied by his knights, he prepared to surround his adversaries but was unable to locate any of them. Then we arrived at
Coxon, a bountiful place stocked with all necessities for our
existence.[40] The Christian inhabitants of Coxon forthwith
turned their city over to the crusaders, who remained there
for three days fully recuperating in the plentiful land.

At this time Raymond of Saint-Gilles, after receiving reports
that the defenders of Antioch had vacated the city, held a council
with his Provençals and made plans to send his knights to guard
Antioch with great care. Finally he chose those whom he wished
to go; namely, Peter, Viscount of Castillon, Peter of Roaix, and
Peter Raymond of Hautpoul, along with five hundred knights.[41]
On their arrival in a valley near Antioch, they learned at a
castle of the Paulicians that the Turks were within the walls of
the city prepared to go all-out in its defense. Peter of Roaix left
the expeditionary force and, under the cover of darkness, passed
near Antioch and without incident entered the valley of Rugia,[42]
where he found and battled Turks and Saracens, killing many

37 The town was Comana or Placentia, a place which is now abandoned.
The army arrived on October 3, 1097; H Chr. 188.
38 Peter of Aulps was a Provençal knight, department of Var, who had
been in the service of Robert Guiscard and later that of Alexius. Runciman,
1951: p. 191. Runciman suggests that Peter was the choice of Taticius.
39 See Bréhier, Gesta, p. 61, fn. 8, for a discussion of the oath.
40 Coxon (Göksun) was inhabited by Armenians. The Christians arrived
October 5 and 6, 1097; H Chr. 190.
41 Peter, Viscount of Castillon, was probably from southern France (Gironde
Dept.). Castillon was south southwest of Toulouse. See Hagenmeyer, Gesta,
p. 232, fn. 26. Peter of Roaix (Vaucluse) was from Roaix in southern France
near Avignon. Peter Raymond Hautpoul (Alto Pullo) was a vassal of the Count
of Saint-Gilles. His castle was near Narbonne and Carcassone. See Raymond
d'Aguilers, p. 52, fn. 2. Modern historians have used the diversionary move of
Raymond to accuse him of wanting to seize Antioch for himself. See our
Raymond IV, pp. 64, 65. Raymond dispatched the force on October 7, 1097;
H Chr. 191. One Tudebode variant writes of Aralium vicecomitem returning
with a spear strung with Turkish noses and lips.
42 Rugia was a valley east of Antioch on the road to Aleppo.

and ardently chasing the remnants. The Armenian dwellers of the land were so impressed by his formidable victory over the pagans that they promptly put themselves under his protection; whereupon he seized the city of Rusa and many castles.[43]

We, who had remained at Coxon, departed and began to climb a devilish mountain so high and with such narrow defiles that no one dared to pass another on the traillike mountain passes.[44] Horses plunged over cliffs and pack animals tumbled over one another as tearful knights stood everywhere wringing their hands, overcome by grief and shock. Doubtful of the fate of themselves and their arms, they sold their shields, expensive breastplates, and helmets for three or five denarii or more, if possible. Those who could not sell their worthless arms threw them down and marched on. Leaving the devilish mountain we came to Marash.[45] The inhabitants of this town met us joyfully outside the walls and brought ample supplies. Here in the midst of plenty we awaited the arrival of Bohemond.

Our knights then came and neared the valley in which the magnificent city of Antioch is located.[46] Antioch is the capital of all Syria. Lord Jesus Christ handed it over to Saint Peter,[47] foremost of the apostles, that he might return it to the veneration of the true faith, which lives and reigns in the triune God for eternity. Amen.[48]

[43] Bréhier thinks that Rusa is perhaps the modern Ruweha. See Bréhier, *Gesta*, p. 63, fn. 10.

[44] The devilish mountain was probably a part of the Anti-Taurus range. See Runciman, 1951: p. 192. The description of the crusaders' plight is in the language of a cleric. *Plaudebant manibus* ("*Prophetia Ezechielis*" 21:17) and *tristitia* (*Evangelium Secundum Joannem* 16:20) are two examples.

[45] Marash was controlled by Armenians. It was governed by Tatoul, a former imperial official. The army arrived here on October 13, 1097; *H Chr.* 194.

[46] The crusaders entered the valley of the Orontes between October 20 and 22, 1097: *H Chr.* 201-204.

[47] There is a question of Peter being the first bishop of Antioch. See Hagenmeyer, *Gesta*, p. 238, fn. 56; See Fulcher, ed. Fink, 1969: p. 93, fn. 3.

[48] Lives and reigns in the triune God (*qui vivit et regnat*); see *Troper*, p. 61; Psalter, Sunday at Prime, Prayer.

IV. The Early Siege of Antioch

As we approached the Farfar entrance, our scouts in their customary reconnoitering found a large Turkish army of reinforcements for Antioch massed against us.[1] Of one accord our men rushed upon them skillfully and overwhelmed their adversaries decisively.[2] Thrown into panic, the barbarians fled in wild abandon and left many dead on the field of battle. Having overpowered them with God's help,[3] our troops seized much loot, horses, camels, mules, and asses loaded with grain and wine. Shortly thereafter our main army moved up and encamped on the banks of the river, and soon the skilled Bohemond with four thousand knights took position before the gate of Antioch to prevent anyone who by chance might try a secret exit or entrance to the city.

On the following day, October 21, 1097, at midday the crusaders arrived before Antioch and placed a strangle hold on three sides of the city, since a tall and very steep mountain prevented a blockade from the fourth side.[4] The hostile Turks within Antioch were so frightened that for almost fifteen days they did not harass any of our men. Soon we were ensconced in the neighborhood, where we found vineyards everywhere, pits filled with grain, apple trees heavy with fruit for tasty eating, as well as many other healthy foods. Although they had wives in Antioch, the Armenians and Syrians would leave the city under pretense of flight and would come to our camp almost every day. They slyly investigated us, our resources, and our strength and then reported on all that they had seen to the

[1] The *portum farreum* refers to the Orontes, *Far* and *Fer*; Albert of Aachen associated it with the idea of iron. See Bréhier, *Gesta*, p. 66, n. 1.

[2] The writer uses Paul's idea of common accord to express the unity of attack. See *Epistola B. Pauli Apostoli ad Ephesios* 6:10-18.

[3] With the aid of God (*adjuvante*) is common in church service. See Missal, 4th Sunday after Epiphany, Prayer.

[4] See Hagenmeyer, *Gesta,* for a discussion of the mountain. Four hundred towers protected Antioch. The Gate of Saint Paul to Aleppo, the Gate of Saint George to Latakia, and the Bridge Gate to Saint Simeon were the main entrances. Raymond d'Aguilers was so impressed with the fortifications that he wrote that Antioch "may dread neither the attack of machine nor the assault of man even if all mankind gathered to besiege it." See Raymond d'Aguilers, p. 31.

accursed Antiochians. After the Turks had been briefed on our situation and plans, they gradually slipped out of Antioch and harassed our pilgrims everywhere and, not restricting themselves to one sector, they made guerrilla attacks from sea to mountain.[5]

In the vicinity of the enemy there was Hārim, a castle where many of the most daring Turks, I say not a few but many, often gathered and made raids on our troops.[6] Indeed our leaders were grief stricken when they received reports that the Turks in many areas mutilated and killed our pilgrims.[7] They dispatched some knights who carefully combed the place for Turks, and after discovery of them our men pressed close and attacked. But gradually they began to retreat to a place where they knew that Bohemond lay hidden with his troops. Soon the Turks killed many of our knights; and thereafter when news of such reached Bohemond, that most courageous athlete of Christ charged out and struck the pagans. However, the Turks, encouraged by our limited numbers, engaged us in combat. The Christians killed many of the enemy and led the captives before a gate of Antioch, where they decapitated them so as to bring sorrow to the Antiochians.[8]

At this time some of the besieged climbed a gate above us and rained arrows into the camp of Bohemond.[9] In the course of this action one woman lay dead from the wound of a speedy

[5] The Bongars text of the *Gesta* and Tudebode have variants which are not in some of the *Gesta* manuscripts. Bréhier, who believes in an original and pure text, explains discrepancies by maintaining that such additions are interpolations. See Bréhier, *Gesta*, p. xxix.

[6] The chroniclers called the garrison, Hārim, Aregh. Hārim was eight miles from Antioch.

[7] All of the *Gesta* texts comment on the fact that the leaders grieved (*nimis doluerunt*), but they do not state as does Tudebode that the Turks mutilated and killed pilgrims. The *Gesta* has the leaders grief stricken because the Turks *conturbabant nostros*. In this case the Tudebode version is more believable in that the mutilation and killing of pilgrims caused grief. See Bréhier, *Gesta*, p. 68.

[8] The *Gesta* states that the Turks killed two knights. Tudebode states that they killed many. See Bréhier, *Gesta*, p. 68. The encounter took place on November 18, 1097; *H Chr.* 211.

[9] Tudebode states that the Turks "climbed a gate (*portam*)." Variants use *in quadam montaneam*. Raymond d'Aguilers writes *de monticulo facultatem sagittandi*. The *Gesta* uses *in quamdam portam*. See *Liber*, p. 50; Bréhier, *Gesta*, p. 70.

arrow. Our leaders then assembled and arranged a council,[10] saying: "Let us build a castle on top of the mountain which rises above the enemies of Bohemond, and thereby we can remain secure and safe without fear of the Turks." Upon completion and fortification of the fort, our leaders took turns guarding it.

Now before Christmas grain and all victuals became very scarce. But we were afraid to stray far, and we found no food in Christian lands, and no one had the courage to forage in Saracen lands without a large host. At length our leaders called a council with the purpose of determining the way to set things right for the people.[11] The council in turn decided that one contingent should search diligently for provisions as well as guard the army on all sides while the other group remained to watch the enemy closely.

Then Bohemond first spoke and said: "Lords and most wise knights, if you favor it and the plan seems desirable and good, I shall go along with the most able Count of Flanders." So following a most glorious celebration of Christmas, on Monday, the second day of the week, Bohemond and the Count of Flanders, along with twenty thousand knights and three thousand footmen, marched safely and untouched into Saracen territory.[12] In fact, many Turks, Arabs, and Saracens from Jerusalem, Damascus, Aleppo, and innumerable other places had assembled en route to lift the siege of Antioch.[13] On news of

---

[10] The *Gesta* calls the castle Maregart. Tudebode does not name the fort. Rosalind Hill thinks that it was a slang expression for Bad Look. See Bréhier, *Gesta,* p. 70; *Gesta,* ed. R. Hill, 1962: p. 30. The leaders assembled on November 23, 1097; *H Chr.* 212.

[11] Bréhier seems to think that it was strange for crusading chiefs to adopt a joint plan. See Bréhier, *Gesta,* p. 71 fn. 5. See our article, Hill and Hill, 1954. Godfrey was ill, the Count of Normandy was absent; Raymond and Adhémar guarded the camp. Raymond d'Aguilers has the crusaders going into Hispania, which was pagan land; Raymond d'Aguilers, p. 33. The council met on December 23, 1097, *H Chr.* 217. The expedition moved out on December 28, 1097, to January 1, 1098; *H Chr.* 219.

[12] Tudebode has twenty thousand knights and three thousand footmen. The *Gesta* has twenty thousand knights and footmen. See Bréhier, *Gesta,* p. 72.

[13] Shams-ad-Daulah, the son of Yaghi Siyan, the governor of Antioch, had enlisted the aid of Dukak, Selchükid ruler of Damascus and Tughtigin, atabeg of Damascus. Raymond d'Aguilers, a cleric, has a better description of the encounters than the *Gesta.* It is strange if the author of the *Gesta* was a Norman knight, that he would have overlooked such an important battle as a vehicle for glorifying Bohemond.

the Christian expedition into their land, the Turks at once
made battle plans and at daybreak approached our united army.
Thereupon they broke into two ranks and attempted to surround us from the vanguard and the rearguard.

Now the famous Count of Flanders, protected on all sides by
faith and the insignia of the Cross,[14] which incidentally he faithfully wore every day, accompanied by Bohemond, rushed against
the Turkish mob. Our troops, in close order, struck the enemy,
who immediately took to heel and fled hastily in panic, leaving
many dead on the battlefield, as well as many horses and great
booty which fell into our hands. The survivors rapidly fled
hence and, as we think, to perdition.[15] We then returned with
great religious ceremony, praising and glorifying the triune God,
who lives and reigns now and forever. Amen.[16]

In the meantime the Antiochian Turks, those enemies of God
and holy Christianity, after learning of the absence of Lord
Bohemond and the Count of Flanders, swarmed out of the town
and contemptuously moved to attack us. With their knowledge
of the absence of some of our most experienced knights, they
probed the weakest spots in our siege forces and discovered on
Tuesday that they could strike and resist us.[17] The accursed
barbarians stealthily approached and, striking viciously the un-
wary and foolish Christians, killed many knights and footmen.[18]
On this bitter day, the Bishop of the Cathedral of the Holy Mary
of Le Puy lost his seneschal, the carrier and protector of his
banner.[19] In fact, if the river had not flowed between us, the
Turks would have struck our men more often and would have

[14] The idea of being armed with symbols is ecclesiastical. The wearing of
the Cross on armor became symbolical of the cause. See *Armaturam Dei,
loricam justitiae, scutum fidei, galeam salutis, gladium spiritus, Epistola B. Pauli
Apostoli ad Ephesios* 6: 11, 15-17.

[15] The way to hell (*perditionis*). See *Evangelium Secundum Matthaeum* 7:13.

[16] See, *Troper,* p. 61.

[17] The attack took place on December 29, 1097, *H Chr.* 220.

[18] Tudebode uses *pedones* for footmen. The *Gesta* uses it at times but in
this instance uses *peditibus*. Gavigan thinks that *pedones* is an Italian word
which reflects the birthplace of the author of the *Gesta*. He ignores the fact
that the *Gesta* is not consistent in the use of *pedones*. See Gavigan, 1943: p. 11;
Bréhier, *Gesta,* p. 74.

[19] Tudebode gives the name of the Holy Mary of Le Puy. The *Gesta* manuscripts do not carry this information, using only Le Puy. The name of
Adhémar's seneschal is unknown.

inflicted greater damage upon us, for to the camp our men fled in wild flight.[20]

The sage Bohemond returned with his army from Saracen lands and crossed over Tancred's mountain, thinking that by chance he might find portable goods.[21] The army had scoured the land for provisions. Some warriors had been successful, but others had returned without spoils, and so these unfortunate ones hastened to return to camp. At this point Bohemond bellowed forth: "Oh! You unfortunate and most miserable people, You vilest and saddest of all Christians; why turn tail so hurriedly? Halt right now! Halt, I say, until we unite our forces; do not stray as do sheep without a shepherd.[22] If the Turks, who watch and lie in ambush day and night in hope of killing or capturing you, find you are isolated or alone, surely they will now kill you if you scatter in retreat."

Following completion of this speech, the masses considered the proposition pro and con, and Bohemond found himself almost alone; yet with what he could find he returned to his army almost empty handed.[23] In the meantime the Armenians, Syrians, and Greeks learned that our foraging forces had come back destitute. Consequently, after a council, they traveled across mountains and well-known places. There they scoured the countryside, buying grain and other foodstuff which they carried to camp where great famine gripped the besiegers.[24] They sold an ass for eight *hyperpoi,* which is worth one hundred and twenty solidi in denarii. Despite this market many crusaders died because they did not have the money for such inflated prices.[25]

[20] The crusaders fled across the bridge of boats.

[21] The use of Tancred's mountain shows that the writer was writing after the event. It was months later that Tancred was given a mountain fortification to guard. The fact that the *Gesta* uses the same expression reveals that the idea of a diary composed by a Norman knight has flaws. See Bréhier, *Gesta,* p. 74.

[22] The speech of Bohemond uses ecclesiastical tags, as sheep stray without a shepherd (*sicut oves non habentes pastorem*). The words are the same in the *Gesta.* See Bréhier, *Gesta,* p. 76, and *Evangelium Secundum Marcum* 6:34.

[23] The account of the empty handed return of the crusaders parallels Raymond d'Aguilers. See *Liber,* p. 53.

[24] Raymond d'Aguilers also describes the famine. See *Liber,* p. 53.

[25] See Hagenmeyer, *Gesta,* p. 257, fn. 20, for a discussion of *purpuratus hyperperos.* In value it was equal to fifteen solidi of deniers in the West as is evidenced by this account. Hay, according to Raymond d'Aguilers, for a night's

William Carpenter [26] and Peter the Hermit, who were most unhappy and miserable, plotted together and sneaked out of camp. Immediately, Tancred followed their trail, seized them, and led the two back in great disgrace. They gave a pledge under oath to return of their own accord and make amends to all of the leaders. William, a despicable creature, lay all night in Bohemond's tent.[27] The next morning at daybreak William came blushing in shame to Bohemond, who addressed him thus: "Oh! You most miserable and infamous of all Franks. Oh! You most shameful and wicked one in all the provinces of Gaul. Oh! You vilest of all men whom the earth suffers; why did you flee so disgracefully? Perhaps, by this vile act you wished to betray these knights and the army of Christ as you surrendered others in Spain!" [28]

William throughout all the tirade was silent [29] and said not a word. So in a body all of the Franks [30] humbly petitioned that Christian knight, Bohemond,[31] that he desist from further punishment of the deserter. Bohemond then replied: "Because of your brotherly love I shall freely agree to your demands if William with all his heart and mind [32] will swear that he will

---

keep of a horse was equal to seven or eight solidi. This figure shows that fodder for horses was one of the real problems of the crusaders.

[26] William Carpenter was viscount of Melun and Gâtinais and was a relative of Hugh of Vermandois. He rode in the army of Godfrey. The escape took place on January 20, 1098; *H Chr.* 229.

[27] The Tudebode and *Gesta* manuscripts vary here. Neither text is clear on the treatment of Peter the Hermit, but they make William Carpenter the villain.

[28] This passage is typical of what we term ecclesiastical fiction. The speech reminds Hagenmeyer of Liutprand. See Hagenmeyer, *Gesta*, p. 259, fn. 9. The terms are ecclesiastical *Scelus gallorum provincia, scelus mundi;* see Hymn, Matins, Nativity of Saint John the Baptist, Office, June 24; *terra suffert* (*Epistola Ad Corinthios Prima* 13:7, *omnia suffert*); *O nequissime;* see *Epistola Ad Ephesios* 6:16. William had deserted in Spain according to Guibert of Nogent, in *RHC Occ,* 4: p. 174. See *Liber,* p. 13 and fn. 1.

[29] William in the best tradition was silent (*Nullus sermo ex eius ore processit*). See *Evangelium Secundum Lucam* 4:22, *verbis gratiae quae procedebant de ore.*

[30] Bréhier, *Gesta*, p. 78, fn. 2, thinks that *Francigenae* refers to northern Frenchmen. See Raymond d'Aguilers, p. 34, for his explanation.

[31] The *Gesta* relates that Bohemond had a serene countenance (*sereno vultu*). See Bréhier, *Gesta*, p. 78; Canon of the Mass: *Supra quae propitio ac sereno vultu respicere digneris.*

[32] For with all his heart and mind (*toto corde*) see *Evangelium Secundum Matthaeum* 22:37.

never abandon the journey to the Holy Sepulchre in good or bad times, and, furthermore, that Tancred will agree that neither he nor his friends shall harm him." [33]

William at once agreed to these terms, and Bohemond immediately dismissed him. But William was overwhelmed by his great humiliation and soon furtively slipped away from the siege.[34] Thus because of our sins God spread poverty and misery in our ranks. There could not be found in all the crusading army one thousand knights who had good battle steeds.[35]

In the beginning of the crusade the emperor, Alexius, had commissioned Taticius, along with rich and noble knights of his army, to conduct the Franks safely and to recover in fidelity the lands seized by the Turks.[36] Now, when Taticius heard that a Turkish army had struck our forces, he lamented the fact because he thought that all had been killed or had fallen into the hands of the pagans. So devising and fabricating all kinds of lies which he could bring together, he spoke to the Latins as follows:

"Lords and most experienced men; you must see that we are pressed by most dire circumstances and that no aid is forthcoming. Think of this; let me return to Romania, and without a doubt I shall come back to you.[37] In fact, I shall see to it that many ships shall come by sea laden with grain, wine, oil, meat, flour, cheese, and all other necessities. I shall provide a market for horses and shall rapidly send merchandise through the lands of the emperor. Understand I shall swear to the faithful execution of these promises and in this place my tent and my household shall remain, and no one shall be skeptical but shall have complete confidence that I shall soon return." Our enemy de-

---

[33] Tancred promised not to harm William (mali facere); Epistola Ad Corinthios Prima 13:5.

[34] William supposedly returned to the East during the Crusade of 1101. See Hagenmeyer, Gesta, pp. 260-261, fn. 17.

[35] Raymond d'Aguilers gives a similar number and states that the Provençal horses numbered one hundred; Raymond d'Aguilers, p. 37.

[36] Taticius (Teigus, Titidus, Tatic, Tatinus) was the leader of the Byzantine forces and represented Alexius. He had opposed the siege of Antioch. Tudebode states that he went along to recover the lands of the emperor. The Gesta makes no such statement.

[37] The speech of Taticius has a few Biblical tags. Revertar ad vos parallels Prophetia Malachiae 3:7 (Revertar ad vos, dicit Dominus exercituum).

parted, leaving all his goods in camp and perjuring himself now and for eternity.[38]

So after this we were in desperate straits because the Turks put pressure on us everywhere, and no one had the nerve to leave the encampment, so great was the fear of the enemy. They fettered and confined us on one side and then the other so that we were very sad and distraught. Our leaders were in great fear, and the possibility of aid and succor was completely lacking.[39] So the little people along with the miserably poor fled either to Cyprus, Romania, or the mountains.[40] We did not dare go to the sea for fear of the evil Turks, and no road was open to us.

When our leaders heard that a host of Turks was approaching, they held a council [41] and discussed the matter in such a manner: "Let us face it. A great Turkish army is poised to attack us; what shall we do? We are too weak to fight a two-front battle. But we can divide our forces into two parts with one part composed of footmen to guard our tents closely and to restrict the movement of the Antiochians. The other part formed of knights shall forthwith ride out against our enemy, which is bivouacked nearby in the castle Hārim beyond the Orontes bridge."

Late in the day they went from their tents across the river and held a council which declared the following: "We shall go

[38] Taticius left the crusaders in the early part of February; H Chr. 230. The causes of his withdrawal are muddled. Perhaps Anna was correct when she stated that he was frightened by Bohemond. But Raymond reported that he ceded Tursol, Mamistra, and Adana to Bohemond. This statement has been accepted as an error on the part of Raymond. However, if the Tudebode variants were correct in their report of land being ceded in Romania to Bohemond (Romania to the chroniclers was a vague term and could have included Cilicia), then Raymond was not as foolish as moderns have made him. See Raymond d'Aguilers, p. 37, fn. 16.

[39] Raymond d'Aguilers gives a more detailed account of the plight of the crusaders; see Raymond d'Aguilers, pp. 36, 37.

[40] Cyprus was held by the Byzantines.

[41] Tudebode states that the crusading leaders heard of the coming of the Turks and in council worked on plans. The Gesta has Bohemond addressing the group. See Bréhier, Gesta, p. 82. This important variant is overlooked by Tudebode's critics. Why would Tudebode drop Bohemond from his account in view of the fact that he shows no dislike of him? It seems to us that this was a rewrite job of some scribe. It is generally true that chroniclers did not attend council meetings. Ridvan, Selchükid ruler of Aleppo, along with Sokman the Artukid, emir of Amida, and the emir of Hamah led the Turks. Raymond says that the council was held in the house of Adhémar. He ignores Bohemond's speech. The council was held February 8, 1098: H Chr. 232.

against twenty-five thousand of our foes. Adhémar, Robert of Normandy, and Count Eustace shall remain to guard our camp from the besieged Antiochians." [42]

At daybreak they sent from our troops scouts to view the Turkish army and to determine where they were and to be sure what they were doing. These patrols sneaked out and began to search and investigate carefully the hidden location of their adversaries. They saw the scattered Turks coming from part of the river in two groups with their maximum force in the rear. Rushing back they yelled: "Here they come! Get ready! Get ready. The Turks are almost here." [43]

Our troops spread out and each leader formed his own battle order. Six lines were drawn up, five of which, with the Count of Flanders in the lead, rushed against the Turks.[44] In the meantime in the rear, Bohemond advanced slowly with his men. Thus our soldiers took the offensive opportunely and close-handed fighting ensued.[45] The clash of arms echoed to the very heavens and the shower of missiles darkened the elements.[46] Following these preliminaries, the main Turkish division, held in reserve to the rear, launched a savage attack and forced us to retreat slowly.

Grieved by the sight of this retreat, Bohemond ordered his constable, Robert, son of Gerard, in a spirited command: "Remember the wisdom of antiquity, the bravery of your forebears, and, above all, how they made war. Go forth, armed on all sides with the Cross, as the most valorous Christian athletes and, as

[42] Tudebode writes that Adhémar, Robert of Normandy, and Count Eustace would guard Antioch. He also mentions a force of twenty-five thousand Turks. The *Gesta* omits these details. Raymond notes that there were not less than twenty-eight thousand horsemen. See Raymond d'Aguilers, p. 40; Bréhier, *Gesta*, p. 82.

[43] Tudebode omits the rallying speech of Bohemond along with praise of him, which includes *sapiens, prudens, magnus, magnificus, fortis,* and *victor.* See Bréhier, *Gesta,* p. 82. The terms are used widely by churchmen. See Blaise, pp. 198, 256, 270, 336, 615, 616.

[44] Tudebode mentions the role of the Count of Flanders. The *Gesta* ignores the Count of Flanders. Certainly, in the light of the role of the Count of Flanders, this was a serious omission. See Bréhier, *Gesta,* p. 84.

[45] Raymond d'Aguilers has an account which parallels this although he uses the events for a point of departure for ecclesiastical excursions.

[46] The description of the noise of battle is similar in Tudebode and the *Gesta.* Hagenmeyer, *Gesta,* p. 283, fn. 42, thinks that the description is similar to Vergil. *Liber* I *Machabaeorum* 5:31 is a more likely source.

wise and experienced soldiers, strike the enemy while carrying the banner of Bohemond." [47]

The other division, upon the sight of Bohemond's banner being carried so staunchly before them, returned to battle and in a united front struck their foes. The crusaders numbered seven hundred while the Turks had twenty-five thousand.[48] So, the pagans, stunned by the turn of events, broke ranks and at once took to wild flight, only to be pursued closely by the Christians, who overwhelmed and destroyed them as far as the Orontes bridge. The Turks hurriedly returned to the Hārim camp, took all goods in sight, plundered and put to torch the castle, and finally beat a hasty retreat. The Armenians, Syrians, and Greeks, on news of the Turkish disaster, followed them and from ambush killed and captured many of the fugitives. By God's approval on that day our foes were cast down.

The crusaders recovered an adequate number of horses and other essentials. They also led back captives and carried one hundred heads of the slain Turks before a gate at Antioch, where legates of the emir of Babylon, who had been sent to the Count of Saint-Gilles and other lords, were encamped.[49] Meanwhile, the Christians who had remained in camp battled daily with the Turks before three gates of Antioch. The above battle was fought on Tuesday before Ash Wednesday, February the ninth, with the benediction of our Lord Jesus Christ, Who with the Father and the Holy Spirit lives and reigns for eternity.[50] Amen.

[47] The speech to Gerard is longer in the *Gesta* than it is in Tudebode. Bréhier thinks that it was written by a clerk. See Bréhier, *Gesta*, p. 85, fn. 3. The *Gesta* uses the story of the raging lion. Raymond used a similar story; Raymond d'Aguilers, p. 18, fn. 20. *Liber I Machabaeorum* 2:51 is probably Tudebode's source for this account.

[48] The twenty-five thousand is an emendation from variant manuscripts of Tudebode.

[49] Tudebode states that legates of the emir of Babylon were sent to Raymond of Saint-Gilles and the other leaders. The *Gesta* omits this information. Raymond does not state the number of Turkish heads brought back, but he does go into a discourse on God's wisdom.

[50] The battle was fought on February 9, 1098; *H Chr.* 233. See Missal, prayer ending, *qui tecum*.

V. The Later Siege of Antioch

WITH THE HELP of God our soldiers returned celebrating and cheering the victory over the vanquished Turks, who in abject defeat fled willy-nilly, some into Corozan, and others into Saracen lands. Our leaders and lords were aware that the Antiochians harassed and restricted us day and night and that they watched and lay in ambush wherever they could injure or pester us. Consequently the crusaders assembled and in council decided: "Before we lose our army of God, let us build a castle at the mosque which faces the Bridge Gate and there, perhaps, we can immobilize our foes." So they agreed unanimously in council that it was a good proposal.[1]

The Count of Saint-Gilles spoke first and proposed: "Aid me in building the castle, and I shall fortify and protect it."

Bohemond then interjected: "If you wish and the other lords are favorable, I shall go with you to Port Saint Simeon to escort safely the workers there who will certainly build the castle.[2] Those who remain shall be on the alert for defense if our and God's enemies should sneak out of Antioch. In the meantime the entire force shall assemble where we designate." Thus the plan was carried out.

Raymond of Saint-Gilles and Bohemond marched out to Port Saint Simeon. We who remained came together according to instructions to build the fortification. On sight of this activity, the Turks readied themselves and marched out of Antioch in battle array. Soon they swept upon us, routing our forces and causing us great sorrow and pain. On the following day, the Turks, now aware of the absence of the leaders from the siege and of the fact that they had passed to the port, on orders from the high command, launched an attack against the Christians coming from Saint Simeon. When they saw Raymond and Bohemond approaching as an escort for the mechanics, the

---

[1] The description of the site for the building of the castle is given in Raymond d'Aguilers, *Liber*, p. 49. The council was held on March 5, 1098, *H Chr.* 241.

[2] The Port of Saint Simeon, named in honor of the anchorite, was a short distance from Antioch. A fleet carrying English and Italian pilgrims anchored here on March 4, 1098. There is no consensus on the presence of Edgar Aethling. See *H Chr.* 240.

Turks immediately began to hiss and chatter and to scream out in blood curdling cries and at the same time to press in while showering our men with missiles and arrows and wounding and cruelly slashing with their swords.[3]

The Turkish attack was so overwhelming that our men took to their heels over the nearest mountain or the most convenient path; and those who were swift of foot survived, but the laggards met death for the name of Christ.[4] More than one thousand knights or footmen martyred on that day rose joyfully to heaven and, bearing the stole of customary white-robed martyrdom, glorified and praised our triune God in whom they happily triumphed; and they said in unison: "Our God! Why did you not protect our blood which was shed today for your name?"[5]

Following a different road, Bohemond with a few knights gave his horse free rein and sped to the assembled group of beset crusaders. Burning with anger over the death of our men, we invoked the name of Jesus Christ and, being assured of the crusade to the Holy Sepulchre, moved as a united front against our foes and joined in battle with one heart and mind. The Turks, enemies of God and us, stood around stunned and paralyzed with fear because they thought that they could overwhelm and slaughter us as they had done the troops of Raymond and Bohemond.[6]

But Omnipotent God permitted no such thing. Knights of the true God, protected on all sides by the sign of the Cross, rushed pell-mell and courageously struck the Turks. In the ensuing rout the besieged scurried to safety by way of the narrow bridge to Antioch. The survivors, who could not push their way through the jam of people and horses, were snuffed out in everlasting death, and their miserable souls returned to the devil

[3] The approach of the Turks is reminiscent of the description of the battle of Dorylaeum.

[4] This skirmish took place on March 6, 1098; *H Chr.* 243.

[5] The Bongars edition of the *Gesta* parallels Tudebode here. The *Gesta* has a similar ending ("Oh God! Avenge our blood which was shed today for Your name.") after the siege of Nicaea. See Bongars, *Gesta*, p. 13, and Bréhier, *Gesta*, p. 42 and 90, textual note *1*. See *Apocalypsis B. Joannis Apostoli* 6:10. These differences indicate considerable scribal tampering.

[6] The account of Raymond d'Aguilers is more detailed and notes the role of Godfrey. See *Liber*, pp. 60, 61.

and his legions.[7] We knocked them in the head and drove them into the river with our deadly lances so that the waters of the swift Orontes seemed to flow crimson with Turkish blood. If by chance one of them crawled up the bridge posts or struggled to swim to land, he was wounded. All along the river banks we stood pushing and drowning the pagans in the pull of the rapid stream.[8]

The din of battle coupled with the screams of Christians and Turks rang out to the elements, and the rain of missiles and arrows darkened the sky and obscured the daylight.[9] Strident voices within and without Antioch added to the noise. Christian women of Antioch came to loopholes on the battlements, and in their accustomed way secretly applauded as they watched the miserable plight of the Turks.[10] Armenians, Syrians, and Greeks, willingly or unwillingly, by daily orders of the tyrannical Turkish leaders, sped arrows against us.[11] Twelve Turkish emirs in line of duty met death in soul and body as well as fifteen hundred of their most experienced and brave soldiers who were also the core of Antioch's defense.[12]

The survivors in Antioch did not have the *esprit de corps* to shout and gibber by day and night as had been their custom. Only night broke off the skirmishing of crusaders and their opponents and so ended the fighting, the hurling of javelins, the thrusting of spears, and the shooting of arrows. So by the strength of God and the Holy Sepulchre the Turks no longer possessed their former spirit, either in words or deeds. As a result of this day, we refitted ourselves very well in horses and other necessities.

[7] These words are used frequently by ecclesiastics, for example, everlasting death. See Blaise, p. 460; II *Epistola Beati Pauli Apostoli ad Thessalonicenses* 1:9.

[8] Raymond d'Aguilers has a similar but less dramatic account. See Raymond d'Aguilers, pp. 42, 43.

[9] The description repeats a former account of a skirmish. See Bréhier, *Gesta*, p. 84.

[10] Women applauding (*plaudebant manibus*) was the Christian way of approval. See Blaise, p. 127; *Liber Psalmorum* 46:1; *Liber Quartus Regum* 11:12.

[11] Tudebode adds Greeks. The *Gesta* has Armenians and Syrians. See Bréhier, *Gesta*, p. 94.

[12] The number of dead, 1500, is the same number which Raymond gives. Raymond d'Aguilers, p. 44. The encounter took place on March 6, 1098; *H Chr.* 243.

At daylight on the following day, the Turks of the city sneaked out and gathered together all of the rotting bodies of the dead which they could find along the river banks, with the exception of those hidden in the river bed, and buried them at the mosque beyond the bridge, which was in front of the city gate. They buried along with their comrades cloaks, gold bezants, bows, arrows, and many other goods which we cannot name.

Our men immediately made preparations after receiving news of the burial of their foes and hastened to the diabolical chapel, where they duly ordered the corpses to be dug up, the tombs smashed, and the cadavers to be pulled out of their graves. They then tossed all of the bodies into a pit and carried the decapitated heads to their tents. Thus they had a perfect count of the casualties with the exception of four horse loads of heads carried to the lieutenants of the Emir of Cairo, who were encamped by the sea. The sight of this action caused the Turks to be dejected and grief-stricken almost to death, and daily they did nothing but weep and wail.[13]

On the third day following, happy and boastful we came together to build the forenamed castle with stones drawn from the tombs of the Turkish dead. Upon completion of the fort, we soon very skillfully put a strangle-hold on the besieged, whose inflated arrogance was brought to nil. Each of our leaders strengthened the castle with a huge breastwork and wall, and they built on it two towers at the site of the mosque. Safely we rambled hither and thither to the port or to the mountain, praising and glorifying pleasantly and joyfully in one harmonious voice our Lord God to Whom is the honor and the glory throughout all eternity.[14]

All of our leaders and princes entrusted the protection of the castle to Raymond of Saint-Gilles because he had more knights

---

[13] The story of the carrying of the heads of the Turks to the representatives of the emir of Cairo parallels the account of Raymond. See Raymond d'Aguilers, pp. 40, 41.

[14] The *Gesta* manuscripts omit details of the strengthening of the castle. The fortification was called *La Mahomerie*. See Bréhier, *Gesta*, p. 96. Work was started on March 8, 1098, and completed by the nineteenth or twentieth; *H Chr.* 248. Tudebode's ending of the episode in what some writers call a doxology varies from the *Gesta* manuscripts.

in his household and also more to give.[15] He guarded the fort with his troops and the following leaders: Gaston of Béarn with his men; Viscount Peter of Castillon; Viscount Raymond of Turenne; William of Montpellier; Gouffier of Lastours; Peter Raymond of Hautpoul; and William of Sabran.[16] These and many more, along with his following, were with the count.

Raymond of Saint-Gilles secured knights and retainers through either wealth or compacts for the purpose of protecting the castle. One day the Turks came to the fort and after surrounding it on all sides screamed, shot volleys of arrows, and wounded and killed our defenders. Thus our camp was pinned down by arrow fire, and had not reinforcements from the other army come, great harm would have befallen them.[17]

After this scene our leaders planned and made a great mole with which they could bore through the bridge. This done, from dawn on a certain day they battled above the bridge and dragged forward the mole. Many Turks were killed and the bridge was penetrated. At nightfall as our men lay asleep, the Turks of the city sneaked out, burned the mole, and restored the bridge, much to the great irritation of the Christian army.[18]

[15] The manuscripts of the Gesta omit the choice of Raymond to guard the castle and all details of events connected with it. Raymond d'Aguilers indicates that the Count of Saint-Gilles took charge of the castle contrary to the wishes of some of his followers. However, he uses the incident for ecclesiastical lessons on sloth and avarice. He likewise does not give the names of Raymond's men. See Raymond d'Aguilers, p. 44. Hagenmeyer and Bréhier do not explain the lacuna in the Gesta. They also fail to give Tudebode credit for information which Raymond does not furnish.

[16] Viscount Peter of Castillon; see note 41, chap. III; Peter Raymond of Hautpoul; see note 41, chap. III; Gaston of Béarn was a viscount of Béarn, Oloron, and Montaner and was also lord of Sargossa; see Jaurgain, 1902: 2. William of Montpellier was William V, Lord of Montpellier. He had been protected by Raymond when he was young. He made two trips to the Holy Land and also participated in the siege of Majorca. See HGL 3: pp. 389, 577, 621, 622. Gouffier of Lastours was Lord of Lastours near Nexon (Haute-Vienne). He was originally from Limousin. See Notitiae duae Lemovicenses, in RHC Occ 5: p. 351; L'Abbé Arbellot, 1881, pp. 10, 11; William of Sabran was Lord of Sabran(Gard) and one of the leading noblemen of the Diocese of Uzès. He was in the Provençal army; see HGL 3: pp. 490, 491; V, col. 687, 708, 732. Raymond of Torena(Tudebode), Raymond of Tentoria(Gesta) was the Viscount of Turenne in the Limousin; see Arbellot, 1881: p. 11; Bréhier, Gesta, p. 185, fn. 5.

[17] This account parallels the story of Raymond d'Aguilers; see Raymond d'Aguilers, p. 45.

[18] Tudebode has information here that is recorded neither by Raymond nor by the Gesta. His critics again ignore this fact.

On another day the Turks led to the top of an Antiochian wall a noble knight, Rainald Porchet, whom they had imprisoned in a foul dungeon.[19] They then told him that he should inquire from the Christian pilgrims how much they would pay for his ransom before he lost his head. From the heights of the wall Rainald addressed the leaders: "My lords, it matters not if I die, and I pray you, my brothers, that you pay no ransom for me. But be certain in the faith of Christ and the Holy Sepulchre that God is with you and shall be forever. You have slain all the leaders and the bravest men of Antioch; namely, twelve emirs and fifteen thousand noblemen, and no one remains to give battle with you or to defend the city."

The Turks asked what Rainald had said. The interpreter replied: "Nothing good concerning you was said."

The emir, Yaghi Siyan, immediately ordered him to descend from the wall and spoke to him through an interpreter: "Rainald, do you wish to enjoy life honorably with us?"

Rainald replied: "How can I live honorably with you without sinning?"

The emir answered: "Deny your God, whom you worship and believe, and accept Mohammed and our other gods. If you do so we shall give to you all that you desire such as gold, horses, mules, and many other worldly goods which you wish, as well as wives and inheritances; and we shall enrich you with great lands."

Rainald replied to the emir: "Give me time for consideration;" and the emir gladly agreed. Rainald with clasped hands knelt in prayer to the east; humbly he asked God that He come

---

[19] The story of the martyrdom of Porchet does not appear in Raymond or the *Gesta*. The *Chanson d'Antioche* uses the story for dramatic effect. Tudebode uses the story for the same reason but makes an effort to give an historical background. He uses the figure of twelve emirs and fifteen thousand noblemen meeting death. These figures had been given earlier. The temptation of Porchet, like that of Christ by Satan, was popular in saints lives. Porchet prayed with clasped hands (*iunctus manibus*). This was a common prayer attitude. Porchet implored God (*rogans ut subveniat*) to come to his aid in good church style. See Blaise, pp. 185, 197, 198, 201. Tudebode also has the soul of Porchet to be drawn to the bosom of Abraham. See *Evangelium Secundum Lucam* 16:22; *The Testament of Abraham*, ed. Barnes, 1892; pp. 72, 73. Lazarus was received into the bosom of Abraham; (Abraham's bosom is depicted in art on the west portal of Saint Trophimus at Arles). Porchet was captured March 6, 1098; *H Chr.* 244.

to his aid and transport with dignity his soul to the bosom of Abraham.

When the emir saw Rainald in prayer, he called his interpreter and said to him: "What was Rainald's answer?"

The interpreter then said: "He completely denies your god. He also refuses your worldly goods and your gods."

After hearing this report, the emir was extremely irritated and ordered the immediate beheading of Rainald, and so the Turks with great pleasure chopped off his head. Swiftly the angels, joyfully singing the Psalms of David, bore his soul and lifted it before the sight of God for Whose love he had undergone martyrdom.

Then the emir, in a towering rage because he could not make Rainald turn apostate, at once ordered all the pilgrims in Antioch to be brought before him with their hands bound behind their backs. When they had come before him, he ordered them stripped stark naked, and as they stood in the nude he commanded that they be bound with ropes in a circle. He then had chaff, firewood, and hay piled around them, and finally as enemies of God he ordered them put to the torch.

The Christians, those knights of Christ, shrieked and screamed so that their voices resounded in heaven to God for whose love their flesh and bones were cremated; and so they all entered martyrdom on this day wearing in heaven their white stoles before the Lord,[20] for Whom they had so loyally suffered in the reign of our Lord Jesus Christ, to Whom is the honor and glory now and throughout eternity. Amen.

Now all the trails used by the Turks were blocked and cut off with the exception of a part of the Orontes where a castle and a monastery were located.[21] If this castle had been impregnable, no one would have had the courage to sally out of the city gate. Consequently, our men met in council and unanimously said: "Let us pick someone from our number who can hold the fort steadfastly and can effectively block the enemy from the mountain, the plain, and the entrance and exit to Antioch." Many

---

[20] See *Apocalypsis B. Joannis Apostoli* 7: 9-17; Breviary(Antiphon) Second Vespers, November 1.

[21] The castle was located near a castle and monastery of Saint George on Mount Cassius. It was called Tancred's mountain.

refused to pitch camp there unless united action was taken.[22]

Then Tancred first came forward and offered: "If I have the assurance that it will be advantageous to me, I shall not only zealously strengthen the castle with my troops, but I shall energetically deny the way by which our enemies have so frequently worried us."

Immediately the council pledged four hundred marks of silver.[23] Tancred then responded forthwith, and alone with his most distinguished knights and followers moved out and soon thereafter blocked the road and the path so that none of them, already terrified by Tancred, dared to go outside the gate of Antioch for fodder, wood, or other essential goods.

Tancred kept his position there at the castle along with his men and began a tight hold on Antioch. On the same day a large number of Armenians and Syrians came securely from the mountains packing provisions for the assistance of the beleaguered Turks in Antioch. Tancred intercepted them and at once seized the traders and all of their pack train, which carried grain, wine, barley, oil, and like goods. Thus Tancred conducted affairs so vigorously and fortunately that he had all paths blocked and cut off until Antioch was captured.

[22] Only the Bongars *Gesta* and Tudebode mention the refusal of some leaders to garrison the fort. Hagenmeyer, *Gesta,* p. 290, follows Bongars here. The council was held on April 5, 1098; *H Chr.* p. 256.

[23] Raymond of Saint-Gilles contributed one hundred marks to the Tancred fund. On the value of this contribution see Bréhier, *Gesta,* p. 99, fn. 2: Raymond d'Aguilers, p. 46.

VI. The Capture of Antioch and Kerbogha's Siege

ALL OF THE EVENTS which occurred before the capture of Antioch I can neither name nor relate; consequently, I shall hereafter write of a few. I suggest that there is no person in this area, be he clerk or layman, who could in every respect either orally or in writing record the true events. There was a Turkish emir, Fīrūz, who became very friendly with Bohemond.[1] Often through mutual messengers Bohemond suggested that Fīrūz admit him to Antioch; and, in turn, the Norman offered him the Christian religion along with great wealth from many possessions. Fīrūz, in accepting these provisions, replied: "I pledge freely the delivery of three towers of which I am a custodian, and I shall turn them over voluntarily at whatever hour he wishes."

Bohemond, now sure of entrance into Antioch, and delighted over his plan, came before the leaders with a calm expression and an assured mind and confidently brought forth the happy proposal in these words:[2] "Men! Most experienced knights! You see how all of us, great and small, are exposed to abject poverty and are dismally ignorant of the means by which our fortune may change for the better. If this plan seems advantageous and fair, then let one from your ranks, chosen by you, set himself as leader; and if he can acquire Antioch by any clever method, or by himself, or through the help of others devise Antioch's fall, let us unanimously agree to give it to him."[3]

---

[1] Fīrūz was called Pirus, Pyrus, Pyrrhus, Firous, Feirus, and other names. Raymond d'Aguilers called him a Turk with the exception of manuscript B, which called him a Turcatus. Rosalind Hill accepts this variant and thinks that he was a renegade Turk. Fulcher thinks that he was an Armenian who became a Muslim. See Fulcher, ed. Fink, 1969: p. 98, fn. 1; Raymond d'Aguilers, p. 46, fn. 16; p. 47, fn. 1. Bréhier accepts Guibert's versions of the activities of Fīrūz after the fall of Antioch. Bréhier, Gesta, p. 101, fn. 4.

[2] Bohemond came with placido vultu. See Missal, Postcommunion, Most Holy Name of Jesus (Sunday between the Circumcision and Epiphany).

[3] The Gesta and Tudebode use ingenio and ingeniare. Bréhier uses ingeniare to mean an assault on Antioch. In their context they read more like a southern French oath and we have so translated. See HGL 5; cols. 223, 301 and also see c. 410, sine fraude et nullo malo ingenio (vernacular no t'en enganare). See Bréhier, Gesta, p. 101, fn. 5.

All the leaders rejected and blocked the scheme and said: "No one shall be given the city and all shall possess it equally. Since we have toiled equally, we shall share equally its possessions." [4] Following this reaction, a scowling Bohemond immediately turned heel on the dissenters.

Shortly thereafter all of our leaders received news of an enemy army composed of Turks, Publicans, Agulani, Azymites, and many other nations of people whom I can neither number nor identify.[5] Forthwith our commanders assembled and in council concluded: "If Bohemond can seize Antioch either through himself or others, we shall of our own free will give it to him on the condition that, if Alexius should come to our aid and should wish to carry out all the conventions which he promised and pledged to us, we shall return Antioch in accordance with justice. If Alexius does not do so, Bohemond shall have eternal possession." [6]

Bohemond wasted no time and daily began to make humble requests of his friend, Fīrūz, and to give assurances with abject promises and saccharine words in the following manner: "It is now the proper time to carry out our plan; therefore my friend, Fīrūz, help me."

Fīrūz was pleased with Bohemond's message and said: "I will aid in all commitments which I am obligated to carry out." On the next night [7] Fīrūz sneaked his son to Bohemond to give him greater assurance of his entrance to Antioch. Then he sent the following message: "Have the heralds blow their trumpets and

[4] We have translated *honorem* to mean possessions. See our article, Hill and Hill, 1953: pp. 322-327. The proposal was made on May 25, 1098; *H Chr.* 260.

[5] Agulani—See fn. 16, chap. III. Publicans were the Paulicians, probably a Manichaean sect, which was very numerous in Armenia. As enemies the Armenians and Maronites were probably the Azymites. The term came from unfermented cakes used by the Jews. It was called lifeless bread. Azymites applies to Latins, Armenians, and Maronites, who celebrated the Holy Eucharist with unleavened bread. See *The Catholic Encyclopedia* 2 (New York, 1907): pp. 171, 172. Publicans and Agulani are mentioned in *La Chanson d'Antioche Provençale* in *Archives de l'Orient Latin* 2: p. 490. The army which was reported was that of Kerbogha, atabeg of Mosul.

[6] Raymond d'Aguilers states that Bohemond was offered Antioch by all of the princes except Raymond of Saint-Gilles in January. See Raymond d'Aguilers, p. 37. The acceptance of Bohemond's proposal was on May 29, 1098; *H Chr.* 262.

[7] Probably June 2, 1098; *H Chr.* 264.

assemble the Frankish people so that they may rush forth and pretend to ravage Saracen lands, and afterwards return rapidly by the mountain on the left. I shall be on the lookout ready for these troops, whom I shall conduct safely into the towers which I guard." [8]

Then Bohemond at once summoned a sergeant, Big Crown, and instructed him as a herald to proclaim immediately his order to the Frankish army to prepare for a march into Saracen lands. So it was done. Soon after this Bohemond revealed his plans to Duke Godfrey, the Count of Flanders, the Count of Saint-Gilles, and the Bishop of Le Puy and told them, "If God wills, on this night Antioch will fall to us." With the completion of instructions the knights took to the plain and the footmen to the mountain, and all night they maneuvered and marched until almost daybreak, when they came to the towers which Fīrūz guarded. [9]

Bohemond immediately dismounted and addressed the group: "Go in dare-devil spirit and great *elan,* and mount the ladder into Antioch, which shall soon be in our hands if God so wills." They then went to a ladder, which was raised and lashed to the walls of the city, and almost sixty of our men scaled the ladder and divided their forces in the towers guarded by Fīrūz.

Fīrūz was soon frightened when he saw such a small band of Christians and, apprehensive that he and our soldiers be captured by the Turks, exclaimed, *"Micho francos echome,"* [10] which means "We have few Franks." He further inquired, "Where is Bohemond? Where is that invincible knight?" [11]

In the meantime a southern Italian retainer clambered down the ladder and rushing to Bohemond yelled: "Man! Why do you stand here, wise man? Why did you come here? Behold, we already have three towers."

[8] There are a number of variants in this account. The *Gesta* manuscripts use *dextram montanam* and the Tudebode manuscripts use *sinistram montaneam*. See Bréhier, *Gesta,* p. 104.

[9] June 3, 1098; *H Chr.* 265.

[10] See Bréhier, *Gesta,* p. 106, note *d* and p. 107, fn. 1; The *A* text of Tudebode uses *Micho* and the *Gesta* uses *Micro*. Stylistically, Greek words or phrases were used along with the Latin translation. See Rabanus Maurus, *De Universo,* 420.

[11] Invincible knight (*invictus*), written to describe Bohemond, is frequently used by clerics. See Breviary (Common of a Martyr at Lauds); Hymn, *Invicte Martyr, unicum;* Britt, 1936: p. 328.

Bohemond along with the rest of the crusaders then jumped
to action and *en masse* happily and joyously moved to the ladder.
The occupants of the towers upon seeing the reinforcements
whooped: "God wills it," and we echoed the same.[12] At once
the Christians amazingly began to mount and scale the ladder
to the three towers, and once on top rushed to other towers.[13]
They swiftly dispatched all of the guards of the towers including
the brother of Fīrūz.

In the meantime the scaling ladder by chance broke and
thereby caused such great distress and dejection that we were
soon stunned and saddened. Though the ladder was smashed,
there was a closed gate nearby to our left which was unknown
to some of us because of darkness; but by feeling around and
closely searching where it was hidden, we rushed to it, crashed
down the gate, and poured into Antioch. At once innumerable
shouts broke the silence. The ever active Bohemond commanded that his honorable banner be unfurled on the hill
opposite the citadel, for indeed Antioch was now filled with the
wailing of its inhabitants.[14]

At sunup the crusaders who were outside Antioch in their
tents, upon hearing piercing shrieks arising from the city, raced
out and saw the banner of Bohemond flying high on the hill.
Thereupon they rushed forth and each one speedily came to his
assigned gate and entered Antioch, killing Turks and Saracens
whom they found, with the exception of the fugitives who took
refuge in the citadel. Some Turkish knights fled by way of the
middle gates and saved their lives by flight. Yaghi Siyan, commander of Antioch, in great fear of the Franks, took to heel
along with many of his retainers.[15] In his flight Yaghi Siyan and
his fellows entered the territory of Tancred, which was nearby
Antioch. Because of their worn-out horses, they went into a
village and took refuge in a house. Recognizing Yaghi Siyan,

[12] For *lo*, (*Deus lo vult*) see Grandgent, #391, 392; Schwan-Behrens,
#10 (4a).

[13] Tudebode states that they climbed to three towers. The *Gesta* omits
this detail.

[14] Bohemond's banner was red. Fulcher, ed. Fink, 1969: p. 99; Albert, p. 404.

[15] The details of the capture of Antioch parallel the other accounts. See
Raymond d'Aguilers, pp. 47, 48; Fink, *op. cit.*, pp. 98, 99. Yaghi Siyan was
called Cassianus, Gitcianus, Axoianus, and other names by the chroniclers, He
was governor of Antioch and a father-in-law of Ridvan of Aleppo.

the Armenian and Syrian inhabitants of the mountain seized and
beheaded him on the spot and carried his head to Bohemond,
for which act they received their freedom. In addition, they sold
his sword belt and scabbard for sixty bezants.[16] These events
took place on Thursday, June 3. All of the streets of Antioch
were choked with corpses so that the stench of rotting bodies
was unendurable, and no one could walk the streets without
tripping over a cadaver.

In the past, Yaghi Siyan had often sent a messenger to Kerbogha, military chief of the Persian sultan,[17] while he was still
in Corozan, urging Kerbogha to come at the most opportune
time because a very brave and formidable Frankish army had
Antioch in a vise. Yaghi Siyan went on to promise his immediate surrender of Antioch to Kerbogha or great wealth if help
was forthcoming. Kerbogha began his long journey from Corozan to Antioch soon thereafter, because he had already enlisted
a large army over a long period of time, and he had also received
permission from the caliph, pope of the Moslems, to kill Christians.[18] The emir of Jerusalem with his army, as well as the king
of Damascus with a large contingent, joined forces with him.[19]
Kerbogha also brought together from all parts innumerable
masses of pagans; namely, Turks, Arabs, Saracens, Publicans,
Azymites, Kurds, Persians, Agulani, and many other people
whom I cannot name or number.[20] There were three thousand
Agulani who feared neither lances, arrows, nor arms because
they and their horses were wearing iron armor, and they fought
only with swords.

This horde came to the siege of Antioch intent on scattering
the Frankish invaders. As they approached Antioch, Shams-ad-
Daulah, son of Yaghi Siyan, intercepted them and, rushing into
the presence of Kerbogha, tearfully begged him in these words:
"Oh! Most invincible prince, I humbly pray to you and seek
your judgment with faithful submissiveness as to the extent you
will aid. You can see that the Franks have blocked me on all

---

[16] A bezant was named from *Byzance* and was equal in value to a sou of
gold or a Greek *hyperperos*. See Bréhier, *Gesta*, p. 95, n. 5.

[17] The Selchükid empire was ruled by the Sultan Berkyaruk (1094-1105).

[18] The caliph was the 'Abbāsid Caliph of Bagdad, al-Mustazhir (1094-1118).

[19] Sokman ibn-Artuk joined the forces of Kerbogha. He was emir of Amida.

[20] Kurds were called Curti. They were nomadic people who established
themselves in Syria. See Bréhier, *Gesta*, p. 111, fn. 4.

sides in the citadel of Antioch. They now hold the city, and they demand us to clear out of Romania, Syria, yes, even Corozan. They have achieved all that they wished, once they killed my father, and nothing else remains to them unless they kill me, you, and all yours, and all of our race with the sword. For a long time I have often faithfully awaited your arrival, and I am uncertain if you will help me in this peril."

Kerbogha, in reply, promised: "If you desire my whole-hearted cooperation with you and my loyal help in this peril, then turn over the citadel to me, and you shall see how I shall come to your aid; and I shall place my men to guard the citadel."

Then Shams-ad-Daulah replied to Kerbogha: "If you can kill all of the Franks and chop their heads off and carefully bring them to me, I shall truly give you the before-mentioned citadel; and, finally, I shall pay homage to you and protect the citadel in fealty."

Kerbogha demanded: "It is impossible for you to sit around and think and cogitate. You must surrender the citadel to me at once." So reluctantly Shams-ad-Daulah turned over the citadel to the atabeg of Mosul.[21]

On the third day after we had entered Antioch, the vanguard of our foes made its appearance before the city.[22] Kerbogha's main army had encamped at the Orontes bridge. There they besieged a tower and massacred all of the defenders with the exception of the captain, whom we later found bound in chains after the great battle. On the next day the pagan horde broke camp and moved near Antioch, where it pitched tents between the two streams and remained there for two days.[23]

After the surrender of the citadel, Kerbogha hurriedly sum-

---

[21] The speech of Shams-ad-Daulah is another literary creation of a churchman. Bréhier, who often attempts to make ecclesiastical writings credible, believes that spies could have reported this event. To us this seems highly improbable. The language is couched in clerical words, often from tags in the services. *O invictissime* (Blaise, pp. 219, 232, 233); *supplex precor* (Blaise, pp. 166, 167, 174, 175, 194, 195); *humili devotione* (Blaise, p. 118); *prudentiam* (Blaise, p. 615); *ex toto corde* Breviary (Ordinary, Sunday Office at Nones), Response; *fideliter dabo* is a feudal term. Bréhier, *Gesta,* p. 113, fn. 5.

[22] Kerbogha's main army encamped on June 5, 1098; *H Chr.* 270.

[23] Kerbogha pitched his tents at the confluence on the Orontes and the Kara-Sou (Nahr al-Aswad). He remained here on the sixth and seventh of June; *H. Chr.* 272, 273.

moned one of his emirs [24] whom he knew by reputation to be
a truthful, gentle, and peaceable person, and addressed him: "I
wish you to guard this citadel in fealty to me because I have
recognized for a long time that you are most trustworthy, and
I beseech you to protect it with maximum security. Up to this
point I know that you are very skillful in your work, and I can
find no one of greater veracity and bravery than you."

The emir demurred saying: "I would prefer never to serve
in this capacity; but rather than have a persuasive talk from you,
I shall accept the mission on the condition that I can yield the
citadel if the Franks chase you from the field in deadly
combat." [25]

Kerbogha then acquiesced: "I know that you are so honest and
wise that I consent to whatever beneficial acts you wish to exe-
cute." Then the atabeg of Mosul returned to his army, which
was encamped in a valley. Soon thereafter the Turks, making
sport of the Frankish troops, carried before Kerbogha a very
hideous and worthless sword covered with rust, a wooden bow,
and a most useless lance, which they had taken from some poor
pilgrims.

"Take a look," said these warriors, "at the arms which the
Franks bear in battle against us." [26]

Kerbogha laughed at the sight of the pitiful arms and addressed those in his presence: "These are the warring and
shining arms which the Christians bore to Asia. The Christians
are originally from western lands, by that I mean Europe, which
is a third part of the world.[27] With these arms they think and
are confident they can expel and chase us beyond the borders of
Corozan and blot out our names beyond the rivers of the Amazons.[28] They have already driven out our kinsfolk in Romania

24 Ahmad ibn-Marwān was keeper of the citadel. After the defeat of
Kerbogha, he surrendered the citadel and turned apostate. It is possible he
is the emir in this dialogue. See Hagenmeyer, Gesta, p. 318, fn. 39.

25 The author of this conversation was acquainted with events which took
place after Kerbogha's defeat. Hagenmeyer, Gesta, pp. 318, 319, fn. 44.

26 It was customary for pagans to mock Christians as Christ was mocked.
The whole story is fabricated with the idea of giving interest to the account.
We know of no one who has located the origin of this tale.

27 Tudebode writes that the Christians were from western lands, that is
Europe, a third part of the world. The Gesta does not give this information.
According to legend the world was divided into three parts.

28 The myth of Amazons was well entrenched. They were supposedly
located on the banks of the Thermodon and the Iris (Iechil Irmak). See

and the region of Antioch, the renowned capital of all Syria."

Subsequently Kerbogha called his faithful scribe and ordered: "Scribe, quickly write many letters which are to be read in Corozan, to wit: 'To the Caliph, our pope, and to all the very wise knights of Corozan, greeting and honor without end.[29] Have a good time, carouse and gormandize, scorn and dispute throughout the land. Let everyone indulge in lascivious luxury and again rejoice over siring many sons who will fight valiantly against the Christians. Display widely these three arms which we took from a band of Franks and learn what kind of weapons the Frankish race bears against us.[30] Let them learn, alas, how good and perfect these arms are made to fight against our weapons which are two, three, yes, even four times forged and purified as the purest gold and silver.[31] Tell them that I have all the Franks hemmed in Antioch, for I have free access to the citadel, and they are below in the city. I hold them in my hand, and I shall either kill them or lead them into miserable captivity into Corozan because they threaten to push and drive us beyond the borders of Corozan or to destroy all of ours beyond the rivers of the Amazons or even to throw us beyond upper India, just as they chased all of our relations from Romania and Syria.[32] Henceforth, I swear by Mohammed and the names of all of the gods [33] that I shall not return to your presence until I have captured with my mighty right hand the kingdom of Antioch and all Syria, Bulgaria, yes, even as far as Apulia, to the honor of the gods, of you, and all the offspring of the Turks.' " [34] Thus he concluded his remarks.

Rabanus Maurus, *De Universo*, 343; Bréhier, *Gesta*, p. 117, fn. 1; Hagenmeyer, *Gesta*, p. 319, fn. 52.

[29] The formula is in the style of official Latin letters. This makes the story appear authentic. See *Apocalypsis B. Joannis* 19: 9; Hagenmeyer, *Gesta*, p. 320, fn. 55; Saint Ambrose, *Epistolae, MPL* 16, 914.

[30] Tudebode uses *gens Francia;* the *Gesta* uses *Francigena.* The author of the *Gesta* does not apply the term to northern Frenchmen in this case. See Bréhier, *Gesta*, p. 116.

[31] The story of the purging of the arms appears only in the Bongars edition of the *Gesta* and in Tudebode. See *Prophetia Malachiae* 3:3.

[32] The *Gesta* omits this. If they threw the pagans beyond upper India that would mean that they drove them beyond land. See Rabanus Maurus, *De Universo*, 335.

[33] The Christians had strange ideas that the Mohammedans believed in many gods.

[34] The inclusion of Apulia has led to the conclusion that the writer was Norman. See Hagenmeyer, *Gesta*, p. 322, fn. 69.

VII. Admonitions, Arab and Christian

SHORTLY THEREAFTER, Kerbogha's mother, who was in Aleppo, came to him and tearfully queried: "Son, are the reports I hear true?" [1]

The son countered: "What reports?"

Then his mother said: "I have heard that you wish to fight the Frankish race."

"Then you know the whole truth," replied Kerbogha.

"I call you to witness, son," warned his mother, "through all the names of the gods [2] and through your own great goodness, be not pleased at the thought of immediate combat with the Franks because you are an invincible knight. Indeed, I have never heard a whisper at any time of an imprudent act [3] by you or your army. You have never been seen scurrying from the battlefield before a victor. Your bravery is spread abroad from east to west, and all wise knights tremble at the mention of your name. Son, we know full well that you are a mighty and brave soldier, gifted in the art of war. No people, be they Christian or pagan, can be courageous in your presence. At a whisper of your name, they flee as sheep scatter before the fury of a lion. [4] I beseech you, my most precious and most beloved son, heed my advice and don't stubbornly follow in your decisions, especially your penchant for engaging in battle with the Christians."

Following his mother's admonition Kerbogha heatedly replied: "Mother, what advice is this? I think that you are crazy or possessed by furies. Actually I have more emirs than the Christians have, great or small."

[1] The plea of Kerbogha's mother has created problems for the defenders of the historical accuracy of the *Gesta*. See Bréhier, *Gesta*, pp. vi-vii; Hagenmeyer, *Gesta*, p. 323, fn. 1. They are forced to maintain that this was a camp story repeated by a Norman knight as does Rosalind Hill, 1962: p. 52, or to take Bréhier's view that it was an interpolation by a clerk. In either case a cursory study of the speech reveals a great number of ecclesiastical terms as well as ecclesiastical dramatic writing.

[2] The names of the Gods; see *Liber Psalmorum* 49:1; *Liber Exodi* 23:13. Great goodness; see *Liber Psalmorum* 118:68; *Troper*, p. 21, Blaise, pp. 273, 274.

[3] Imprudent act; see *Epistola Ad Ephesios* 5:17.

[4] The raging lion was frequently a subject of church writing. See *Prophetia Ezechielis* 22:25, *Prophetia Michaeae* 5:8.

His mother, soothing his feelings,[5] answered: "Darling son, the Christians cannot fight you, for I am certain that they are powerless to engage you on the field of battle; but their god battles daily in their ranks and guards them day and night, and keeps watch over them as the shepherd watches over his sheep and permits no people to injure or disturb his flock.[6] If people wish to oppose the Christians, this god of theirs will confound them as he spoke in these words of David: 'Scatter them who do not pray to you.'[7] Indeed before they have made battle plans, the omnipotent and powerful warrior god of the Christians, along with his saints, has immediately conquered their enemies.[8] How much more will he strike you, who are his enemy, all ready to oppose him with all your valor. Dearest one, know this truth: the Christians are called the sons of Christ, and in the words of the prophets they are called sons of adoption and promise.[9] In the words of the prophet, they are the heirs of Christ [10] to whom Christ has already given the promised heritage in these words: 'Your boundaries are from the east to the west,[11] and no one has the audacity to oppose you.' Who can contradict or deny? Certainly, if you launch a war against the Christians, you will be crushed and disgraced. Further, you will lose many loyal soldiers in addition to booty which you and your men have collected, and your lot will be fearful flight. You will not die just now in this war, but you will lose all of your goods in this battle. However, I repeat that you will not die right now.[12] The Christian god, once enraged, does not condemn a culprit at once, but he punishes him with unmistakable retribution. Therefore I

---

[5] The discourse at this point reminds us of Rebekah's conversation with Jacob. See *Liber Genesis* 27; Missal, Third Saturday in Lent.

[6] The shepherd watches over his sheep. See *Prophetia Ezechielis* 34:12; *Prophetia Jeremiae* 31:10.

[7] Scatter them who do not pray to you. See *Liber Psalmorum* 67:2; *Liber Numeri* 10:35. The *Gesta* uses *Liber Psalmorum* 78:6 in addition. See Bréhier, *Gesta*, p. 120.

[8] See note 17, chap. III, and Blaise, pp. 254, 255, for the use of omnipotent in prayers.

[9] Sons of adoption and promise. See *Epistola B. Pauli ad Romanos* 4:13; *Epistola ad Ephesios* 1:5; *Epistola ad Galatas* 4:5, 28.

[10] The heirs of Christ. See *Epistola ad Galatas* 4:7; *Epistola B. Pauli ad Romanos* 8:17.

[11] Your boundaries are from the east to the west. See *Liber Psalmorum* 112:3; Missal, Mass for the Propagation of the Faith (Secret).

[12] Kerbogha died in 1102.

fear lest he enact harsh penance from you, and I say to you now that you will die during this year."

Kerbogha, deeply grieved [13] at his mother's warning, questioned her: "Darling mother, I am curious to know who told you these stories about the Christians: how much their god loves them, how he possesses such great military genius, how they shall overwhelm us in battle at Antioch, how they shall capture great booty, how they shall crush us with a great victory, and lastly how did you learn that I shall suddenly die this year?" [14]

Kerbogha's mother tearfully answered: "Dearest son, you know that more than one hundred years ago it was found in the Koran and in the books of all of the Gentiles that Christendom would march against us and everywhere overwhelm us and rule over the pagans, and that our society would be subjected to the Christians throughout the world; but I do not know when this shall come to pass. I, in my melancholy state, did not hesitate to follow you from the most beautiful city of Aleppo in which I have been watching; and by clever investigating I have gazed upon the stars of heaven. By shrewdly speculating and thoroughly examining with inquisitive mind the planets of the skies and the twelve signs of the zodiac and countless omens, I have concluded the Christian people will overpower us everywhere. I am overwhelmed with sorrow and borne down with melancholy, and I fear that your unhappy mother will survive you." [15]

Kerbogha further inquired: "Darling mother, explain the things which are incredible to me."

In reply she said: "Darling, I shall be glad to do so if I can only know the things which are unbelievable."

Her son replied: "Is it true that Bohemond and Tancred are gods of the Franks and save them from persecution of their enemies? Really, is it true that they eat two thousand cows and four thousand hogs for luncheon?" [16]

---

[13] Deeply grieved (*intimis visceribus*) signifies strong feeling. See Blaise, p. 275.

[14] Sudden death (*morte subitanea*). See *Missale Romanum Mediolani 1474*, 2, 1907: p. 116.

[15] We have not been able to identify these forecasts. The eleventh century put great store in prophecies, and a churchman would be familiar with them as they were a part of his stock stories. Bréhier thinks that these prophecies may be attributed to Daniel, to the sibyls, and to Leon the Sage. He also refers to Liutprand's reference to these tales. See Bréhier, *Gesta*, p. 123, fn. 3.

[16] We are inclined to think that this was a good tale. See Baldricus Dolensis, *Historia Jerosolimitana* in *RHC Occ*, 4, p. 63.

Kerbogha's mother informed him in these words: "Most beloved son, certainly Bohemond and Tancred are mortals just as are the other Christians, but their god bestows greater love upon them than upon any others and daily gives them greater valor in combat than others. Omnipotent is the name of their god, who made heaven and earth and created the sea and the universe in which they live, whose throne in heaven is made in eternity, and whose power strikes fear everywhere." [17]

Her son then committed himself: "Despite these facts, I cannot stop my plans for battle with the Christians."

Upon news of Kerbogha's adamant stand, his very sorrowful mother returned to the city of Aleppo, along with all of the loot which she could collect.

On the third day of the siege Kerbogha made battle preparations, and a large army of Turks accompanied him to the citadel sector.[18] Under the impression that we could match their might, we took up battle positions; but their strength was so awesome that we could not oppose them, and so in disarray we re-entered Antioch. Because of the narrow and cramped gate, many of our fugitives were crushed to death in the jam.[19]

All through this Thursday within and without the walls of Antioch, the Christians fought even until sundown.[20] Likewise, on Friday they battled all day, and the Turks slew many of our men.[21] On this day, Arvedus Tudebodus, a most worthy knight, was wounded. His friends carried him into the city, where he lived until Saturday. On this day between nones and sext he left this world, living now in Christ. His brother, a priest, buried him before the western portal of the church of the blessed Apostle Peter. This brother along with the Christians in Antioch greatly feared death by decapitation. We pray that all readers and listeners give alms and pray for the soul of

[17] Who made heaven and earth. See *Liber Genesis* 2:4; *Liber Exodi* 20:11; Credo.

[18] June 8, 1098; *H Chr.* 275.

[19] Raymond d'Aguilers states that one hundred men lost their lives. There is some question on the location of the fight. See Raymond d'Aguilers, p. 50; Hagenmeyer, *Gesta*, p. 331, fn. 6.

[20] June 10, 1098; *H Chr.* 276.

[21] June 11, 1098; *H Chr.* 280.

Arvedus Tudebodus and for all of the departed souls on the journey to Jerusalem.[22]

On this day William Grandmesnil, his brother Alberic, Ivo of Grandmesnil,[23] William of Bernella,[24] Guido Trosellus and William,[25] brother of Richard, and Lambert the Pauper,[26] overwhelmed by fear after yesterday's battle, which had lasted until vespers, secretly lowered themselves from the walls, and in the dark of night fled on foot to the coast. In the course of their flight they stripped the flesh of their hands and feet to the bone. Others, whose names I do not know, secretly fled with them. Upon their arrival at the port of Saint Simeon where ships were docked, they inquired from the sailors: "Why do you wretches stay here? All of our friends are dead, and we almost lost our lives because the Turkish army has besieged Antioch on all sides."

The sailors, upon receipt of this news, stood dumfounded and overwhelmed with fear and therewith rushed to their ships and sailed away. At this time the Turks arrived upon the scene and killed the Christians whom they found, put to torch the ships anchored in the mouth of the river, and seized their goods. We who remained in the city could not equal the power and arms of the Turks, and so we built between the citadel and us a wall which we guarded day and night. In the meantime we were so

[22] This information is omitted by the *Gesta*. Raymond d'Aguilers has no mention of it. The mention of Arvedus, supposedly a brother of the author, attests to the personal participation of Tudebode in the crusade.

[23] William of Grandmesnil came from Grand-Mesnil or Grandmenil, in the area of Lisieux. His brother was named Alberic (Aubri). We do not know how important Ivo of Grandmesnil was.

[24] William of Bernella (Bernevilla, Barnavilla) possibly came from Barneville-sur- Mer(Manche).

[25] Guido Trosellus was probably Guy I Trousseau from Montlhéry, a village south of Paris. William, the brother of Richard, we have not identified. Guy was called the Red by Ralph of Caen.

[26] Lambert the Pauper has been identified as the Count of Clermont located near Liége. The *Gesta* omits Ivo of Grandmesnil, William of Bernella, and William, brother of Richard. These omissions of the *Gesta* are difficult for Tudebode critics to explain. Bréhier neglects to mention the Tudebode variants and dwells on the variants of the *C* manuscripts of the *Gesta*, which he considers were of a later tradition because they used *dimissi sunt fune*. Tudebode uses *dimissi sunt per murum* as do the *A* manuscripts of the *Gesta*. See Bréhier, p. 127, fn. 7. Raymond d'Aguilers wrote of the deserters lowering themselves from the walls of Antioch by ropes. Later Ordericus Vitalis refers to them as rope dancers. See *Liber*, p. 68. They fled on the night of June 10, 11; *H Chr.* 278.

hungry that we ate horses and asses. Besides we lived in such
mortal terror of the Turks that many of our leading men wished
to flee by night as had the deserters.[27]

One day when our chieftains were assembled on the mountain
before the citadel, grieving and sorrowing and ignorant of what
course of action to take, Stephen, a priest,[28] stepped forward and
said: "Lords, if it pleases listen to my story of what I saw. One
night, as I reclined in the church of Saint Mary, Mother of Our
Lord Jesus Christ, the Saviour of the world appeared before me
accompanied by His Mother, Mary, and Peter, first of the Apostles. The Lord stood before me and said: 'Stephen, do you
recognize me?'[29]

"To whom I replied: 'No.'

"During this conversation a perfect Cross appeared above His
head. Again the Lord interrogated me: 'Stephen, do you recognize me?'

"I answered: 'I could not recognize you except for the fact
that I see a Cross above your head similar to that of our Saviour.'

"The Lord said to me: 'I am your Saviour.'

"At once I fell prostrate, crying and begging humbly that he
aid us against the blockade of this accursed race, which held us
shut up in Antioch. The Lord answered my entreaties as follows: 'I have aided you well, and I continue to assist you greatly.
In fact, I permitted you to take the city of Nicaea and to win all
of your battles; and I have even led you here, suffering along
with you the hardships borne in the siege of Antioch.[30] Furthermore, with timely and great effort I delivered you safe and sound
in Antioch. But many Christians have committed numerous evil

[27] The *Gesta* does not state here that others considered desertion. It notes
that others did desert.

[28] The *Gesta* neglects to mention that the chieftains were gathered on a
mountain but uses *sursum ante castellum*. It does not give the name of the
priest. Tudebode and Raymond call him Stephen. He was probably from
Valence and figured in the visions of Raymond d'Aguilers. He informed the
chieftains on June 11, 1098; *H Chr*. 279. See Bréhier, *Gesta*, p. 128.

[29] The conversation of Stephen is similar to the account in Raymond d'Aguilers. See *Liber*, pp. 72, 73.

[30] The *Gesta* and Tudebode use part of the vision of Peter Bartholomew in
the vision of Stephen when they state that God had given the crusaders Nicaea.
This confusion of the two stories again shows that the author of the *Gesta*
and Tudebode were using Raymond d'Aguilers or a common source. See *Liber*,
p. 86: Brehier, *Gesta*, p. 130.

acts in that they lie with pagan women, and as a result a great stench arises to Heaven.'

"Then the beautiful Virgin Mary and the Blessed Apostle Peter fell before Christ's feet imploring Him that He aid the surviving Christians in their anguish, saying: 'Lord, for a long time the pagan people held our churches, in which they have perpetrated unutterable evil. Indeed if the enemies are expelled by Christians, there will be great happiness among the angels in Heaven.'

"Consequently, the Lord instructed me: 'Stephen, tell my people to turn back to me and I shall return to them; and after five days I shall order the greatest possible aid for the Christians. Each day *Congregati sunt* shall be sung throughout the whole army. Further, Christians shall do penance. They shall in bare feet make processions through the churches and give alms to the poor.[31] The priests shall chant mass and perform communion with the body and blood of Christ. Then they shall begin the battle, and I shall give them the help of Saint George, Saint Theodore, Saint Demetrius, and all the pilgrims who have died on the way to Jerusalem.' [32]

"Truly the Lord said this to me. Oh! my lords, if you have doubts of the truth of this vision, I shall climb a high tower and jump off.[33] If I survive safe and sound, you shall accept my story as true. On the other hand if I am injured in any way, behead me or throw me into the fire." Adhémar forbade the ordeal and commanded the Gospel and the Cross to be brought, and he then made Stephen swear that this was true.

[31] Raymond d'Aguilers cites the *Congregati sunt*. The *Gesta* and Tudebode also use *Congregati sunt*. The use of liturgical materials makes a poor case for a simple Norman knight. The instructions of Stephen resemble the vision of Stephen in Raymond d'Aguilers. God promises to be merciful and return in five days. Peter Desiderius, in reporting a later vision, instructed the crusaders to go in bare feet around Jerusalem. See *Liber*, p. 73, fns. 4, 5; Raymond d'Aguilers, pp. 56, 122; Bréhier, *Gesta*, p. 130.

[32] In a later vision of Peter Bartholomew, the departed were supposed to fight in the coming battle. See Raymond d'Aguilers, p. 60. Saint George was probably martyred in Nicomedia about A.D. 300. His bones were translated to Lydda, his birthplace. Saint Theodore mentioned here was probably Saint Theodore of Amasea, a young soldier saint. There was a Theodore Stratolates who died in A.D. 319 and became a patron saint of Asia Minor. See *English Kalenders*, ed. Wormwald, 1934: pp. 22, 54, 136, 166, *passim*. Saint Demetrius was a patron saint of Bulgaria. The *Gesta* omits the promise of saintly help.

[33] Raymond has a similar offer of Stephen but omits his possible beheading. See Raymond d'Aguilers, p. 56.

After this report all of the leaders decided in council at that hour to swear that none would flee from Antioch while alive either to escape death or to preserve life. Bohemond was reported to be the first to so swear, and Duke Godfrey, Robert, Count of Flanders, and other lords followed suit.[34] Tancred, in like manner, promised that as long as he had forty knights with him he would abandon neither the city of Antioch nor the march to Jerusalem.[35] The news of the oath taking greatly revived the morale of the entire Christian army.

Before our capture of Antioch, the Apostle Saint Andrew appeared to Peter Bartholomew, a pilgrim in our army, and addressed him as follows: "Good man, what are you doing?"

"And who might you be?" questioned Bartholomew.

"I am the Apostle Andrew," replied the saintly visitor. "Son, listen to this truth: If you go to the church of Saint Peter after you have entered Antioch, you will find the Lance of Our Saviour, Jesus Christ, with which He was wounded while hanging on the arms of the Cross." After these words Andrew immediately vanished.

Fearful of revealing the admonitions of Saint Andrew, Peter Bartholomew would not relate them to our pilgrims, for he reckoned that he had seen a vision. Saint Andrew soon returned and queried: "Why have you not informed the pilgrims of my instructions?"

"Lord, who will believe this?" replied Peter.

Within minutes Saint Andrew took Peter and carried him into Antioch to the earthly hiding place of the Lance. "See this," Saint Andrew said, as he drew the Lance from the ground and put it into Peter's hands with these words: "This is the Lance of Our Lord Jesus Christ, which I and my brother, the Apostle Peter, buried here. Look at it." Saint Andrew then put it back in place, and afterwards said to Peter Bartholomew, "Return to the army."

---

[34] Tudebode omits Raymond of Saint-Gilles. Raymond d'Aguilers notes that the princes swore not to abandon the siege, but he does not give their names. See Raymond d'Aguilers, p. 56.

[35] Tancred's offer of forty knights is rather interesting. Later in the crusade Raymond d'Aguilers states that Tancred marched out of Ma'arrat-an-Nu'mān with forty knights. This points to the use of common information in different places. See Raymond d'Aguilers, p. 83.

"Lord! How can I go when the Turks on top of the walls of Antioch will kill me on sight?" questioned Peter.

The Apostle then commanded: "Go and fear not." Whereupon Peter began to depart from Antioch, and the Turkish watchmen said nothing to him.[36]

---

[36] The reporting of the visions of Peter Bartholomew is very detailed in Raymond d'Aguilers' account. Tudebode has a better summation of the story than the *Gesta*. In some instances the *Gesta*, Tudebode, and Raymond d'Aguilers have the same words in the conversation of Saint Andrew and Peter Bartholomew. It seems to us that it would be most unusual if the three writers could employ identical wording unless they were using a common source. Of course, the author of the *Gesta* and Tudebode could have copied Raymond. In this case the purity of the *Gesta* is questioned. Examples of common word usage in the three works are: *Quid agis?; Tu quis es?; Ego sum Andreas Apostolus.* The author of the *Gesta* garbles the story when he has Peter Bartholomew addressing Saint Andrew after he has disappeared. See Hagenmeyer, *Gesta*, p. 343, fn. 5. Following the disappearance of Saint Andrew, according to Tudebode, Peter Bartholomew: "Estimabat autem se visum videre. Alia vice quoque venit ad eum sanctus andreas dicens: 'Quare non dixisti peregrinis quod tibi precepi?' Et ille respondit ad eum: 'Domine quis hoc crediderit?'" The Gesta writes, "Estimabat autem se visum videre." Then he omits "Alia vice quoque venit ad eum sanctus andreas," and adds: "Domine quis hoc crediderit?'" It is obvious that the *Gesta* makes no sense. He was either using Tudebode, Raymond, or a common source. See Bréhier, *Gesta*, p. 132.

VIII. Trials, Tribulations, and Christian Victory

THE TURKS in the commanding citadel pressed our troops so vigorously that they surrounded three of our knights on a certain day in a tower which stood before their fort. The pagans rushed out of the citadel and struck the Christians so hard that they could not resist their courageous charge. Two of the wounded crusaders abandoned the tower, but the third one defended himself all day so cleverly from the Turkish attacks that on that occasion he knocked down two Turks at the entrance of the walls with broken spears.[1] In the course of the day three spears broke in his hands. The knight was Hugh le Forsenet [2] of the army of Godfrey of Monte Scaglioso.[3]

Bohemond and Tancred [4] could not induce their men to storm the citadel because they were shut up in houses and reluctant to fight, some because of hunger and some because of fear of the Turks. Bohemond, greatly angered by this inaction, at once ordered the quarters of Yaghi Siyan put to the torch. The crusaders, on viewing the mounting flames fanned by a brisk wind, abandoned the houses and fled with booty, some toward the mountain before the citadel, others to the gate of Raymond of Saint-Gilles, and yet others to the gate of Duke Godfrey, and thus each returned to his unit. In the course of the fire Bohemond was greatly distressed because he feared that the churches of Saint Peter and Saint Mary would burn because the conflagration blazed from the third hour until midnight and burned two thousand churches and homes.[5] In the middle of the night the wind calmed and the fire smouldered out.

---

[1] Tudebode does not write that the knight killed the Turks. The *Gesta* does so. See Bréhier, *Gesta*, p. 136. Raymond d'Aguilers reports a similar fight in which some Turks were killed. See Raymond d'Aguilers, p. 59.

[2] Formations on Old French *forsener* were not uncommon as a sobriquet. *La Chanson de la croisade Albigeoise*, 1931: p. 52, "per gent forsenea"; Appel, 1902: p. 33, "Breto forsenat;" Bartsch, p. 39, "cist hoem est forsenez." The author of the *Gesta* prefers to use *insanus;* Bréhier, p. 136.

[3] Godfrey of Monte Scaglioso was killed at Dorylaeum.

[4] Tudebode writes Bohemond and Tancred. The *Gesta* omits Tancred. See Bréhier, *Gesta*, p. 136.

[5] Bohemond set fire to part of Antioch on June 12, 1098; *H Chr.* 281.

The Turkish force of the citadel fought day and night with us within Antioch, and nothing separated us but force of arms. At one time four emirs, completely clad in gold armor, came out with the Turks, leading horses likewise encased in gold armor to the knee joints. Our men, who were so hard pressed that they had no time to eat bread or to drink water, were so impressed by this sight that they could endure it no longer.[6] So they erected a wall between them and the mountain and built a fortress-like castle and machines of war so that they could be secure.[7]

Another group of Turks was encamped around Antioch in a valley apart from the others. At nightfall fire from the heavens appeared from the west and fell in among the Turkish troops, astonishing both Turks and Christians.[8] At daybreak the Turks, terrified by the celestial fire, fled hither and thither. However, they surrounded us in Antioch so completely that no one dared enter or leave except stealthily by night. Thus we were besieged and oppressed by the other pagans, enemies of God and Blessed Christianity. They numbered three hundred and sixty-five thousand with the exception of the Emir of Jerusalem, who was there with his soldiers, and the King of Damascus, along with his people, as well as the King of Aleppo with his men.[9]

Consequently, the profane enemies of God held us so closely surrounded in Antioch that many of our people starved to death because of high prices. A small loaf of bread cost a bezant of gold,[10] and of the price of wine I shall not speak; there was not

6 The story of the emirs parading in front of the crusaders is not told in the Gesta. Tudebode has the sight of the taunting emirs to cause the crusaders to build a wall. The use of gentuum by the A manuscript and genium by the C manuscript suggests that some vernacular form of Old French genouz (z equals ts) derived from a Vulgar Latin diminutive conjectured as genuculum occurred in the exemplar. See Schwan-Behrens, #103, 2b, #159, #282; Grandgent, #37; Bartsch, p. 31, genuilz; p. 45, genolz.

7 Tudebode has reference to a wall between the crusaders and the citadel. Raymond of Saint-Gilles, who was ill, guarded it with two hundred men. Raymond d'Aguilers, p. 61.

8 Raymond d'Aguilers writes of a star splitting and falling into the Turkish camp. See Raymond d'Aguilers, p. 57. Tudebode uses ignis de caelo, which is used in Liber Quartus Regum 1:10-14. Hagenmeyer thinks that this was a meteor which fell on the night of the thirteenth-fourteenth of June; H Chr. 282.

9 These are fabulous figures.

10 Tudebode writes a bezant of gold. The Gesta writes a bezant. See Bréhier, Gesta, p. 138.

even a jug of it.[11] One hen sold for fifteen solidi, an egg cost
two solidi, a nut brought one denarius, three or four beans were
worth one denarius, and a small goat cost sixty solidi. The belly
of one goat was worth two solidi; the tail of a ram varied in price
from three to nine denari. The tongue of a camel, which is
small, brought four solidi.[12] The crusaders likewise ate and sold
meat of horses and asses. They cooked leaves of figs, vines, and
trees in water and then ate them. Some put the hides of horses,
asses, camels, oxen, and wild buffalo, dried for five or six years,
into water for two nights and a day; and after mingling them
with the water, boiled and ate them.[13] There were many anxie-
ties and hardships suffered in the name of Christ and for the
journey of freeing the Holy Sepulchre; [14] in fact, far more than

[11] *RHC Occ.* 3, note *a*, p. 73, regards this phrase as broken Greek. The
manuscripts at this point are clouded, *CD* giving *uquen grasin* and *B ut quem
grassim*, while *A* gives *unquen grasin*. Both Grangent, #257, and Schwan-
Behrens #27, 1, note the substitution of *g* and *gr* for *c* and *cr*, Schwan-
Behrens noting that this change is particularly true of words of Greek origin
for which the Latin shows *c* and *cr*. The word *grazal* (bowl) occurs in Provençal,
Adams, 1913: p. 191; and *-inus* was a popular suffix in word formation in
Vulgar Latin; Grandgent, #37. The interpretation of *grasin* as an early
vernacular form meaning a kind of vessel is reinforced by *unquen*, which may
be a vernacular formation on *unquam*, which came into Old French with the
meaning of *jamais* and occurred as *unque*, Bartsch, p. 10, or *onques*, Bartsch,
p. 21, the *-s* being the so-called adverbial *s;* Schwan-Behrens, #313. It would
appear that the compiler here borrowed part of a vernacular phrase. In verse
onques is often found preceding a noun: *c'onques congié n'i quist*, Bartsch,
p. 50; *ne prisent onques fin*, Bartsch, p. 51; *c'onques guerre ne fist*, Bartsch,
p. 49; *ne cantat unkes messe*, La Chanson de Roland, Léon Gautier, ed. and
tr., 1887: p. 150.

[12] Some of this information is not in the *Gesta*. Tudebode has by far the
best list of prices. He is not copying Raymond or the *Gesta* in several examples.
He has a goat's stomach worth two solidi. Raymond has a goat's intestines
worth five solidi. See Raymond d'Aguilers, p. 59.

[13] The *Gesta* and Raymond have similar accounts of the cooking and eating
of dried skins. The similarity of the two accounts at this point is another
example of Sybel's error in stating that the two sources do not parallel in
word structure. See Bréhier, *Gesta*, p. 140, Raymond d'Aguilers, p. 59. Only
Tudebode writes of the age of the skins and the preparation of them. Albert
evidently copied Tudebode or his source of information, because he writes of
skins three to six years old. See Albert, p. 412.

[14] Tudebode writes of the journey for freeing the Holy Sepulchre (*via de
liberanda*). The *Gesta* writes of *deliberanda* which makes no sense. Bréhier
notes this but makes no explanation. See Bréhier, *Gesta*, p. 140. *RHC Occ.* 3,
p. 73, follows *B* with *via liberanda* and note 24 gives *deliberanda AC*. Grandgent, #88, notes the use of *de* with the ablative to replace the genitive as
early as Plautus; also, #37, the use of *-anda*, neuter plural of the gerundive, as
a feminine singular. The fact that *de* and *liberanda* are linked in the manu-

I can recount. As servants of God we suffered such tribulations as well as starvation and fear for twenty-six days.[15]

The shameless Stephen of Blois, head of our army, whom our chieftains had elected their leader before the fall of Antioch, under the pretense of an illness basely retired to another camp called Alexandretta.[16] Deprived of life-saving help while besieged in Antioch, we daily expected him to assist us to the best of his ability. Yet, following news of the Turkish encirclement and blockade of us, Stephen sneaked up a nearby mountain,[17] gazed upon countless tents of the foe, and as a result retired. Suddenly he was terror stricken and disgracefully fled in wild flight with his army. Upon arrival in his camp, he stripped it of goods and cowardly returned in haste. Afterwards he came to Alexius at Philomelium,[18] approached him in secret and in private related: "You may as well know the truth. Antioch has fallen, but the citadel has not, and all of our men are so grievously beset that I think that at this moment they have been killed by the Turks. Retreat as rapidly as you can lest they find you and your following."

Then the frightened Basileus summoned Guy,[19] the brother of Bohemond, and others and asked: "Lords, what shall we do? Think about it. All of our soldiers are caught in a severe siege and perhaps in this very hour are dead at Turkish hands or have been led into captivity, at least so this unhappy count and shame-

---

script is of no consequence. Note on the same folio (23) *inaquam, inadiutorio, incivitate, atille,* and *unacum.*

15 "We suffered such tribulations" (*Epistola B. Pauli ad Romanos* 8: 35). The expression shows the author's use of a former quotation.

16 Stephen of Blois was Count of Chartres and Blois. He was married to Adela, daughter of William the Conqueror, and was a brother-in-law of Robert of Normandy. Following his disgrace he returned to the Levant and lost his life at Ramla in 1102. See Brundage, 1960: pp. 380-395. Raymond d'Aguilers notes that Stephen had been chosen as a leader in the expedition but gives few details. The *Gesta* does not speak of Stephen as *caput nostrorum.* See Raymond d'Aguilers, p. 59; Bréhier, *Gesta,* p. 140. Alexandretta (Iskenderun) was a port north of Antioch. Stephen went to Alexandretta on June 2, 1098; *H Chr.* 263.

17 Bréhier identifies the mountain as Djebel-Ahmar. See Bréhier, *Gesta,* p. 141, n. 6.

18 Philomelium (Akshehir) was in Anatolia between Dorylaeum and Iconium. Alexius, according to his promise, was en route to aid the crusaders. See Bréhier for a discussion of a *C* manuscript; Bréhier, *Gesta,* p. 142, n. 1, and *a.*

19 Guy was the son of Robert Guiscard and his second wide, Sykelgaite. He was Bohemond's half-brother.

ful fugitive relates. If you wish, let us retrace our course rapidly
rather than die swiftly as have our allies."

When that most worthy knight, Guy, heard such lies, along
with everyone he began to cry, to shriek, and to beat his breast
violently. Then all of one accord the Christians implored: "Oh!
True and triune God,[20] why did you permit this to happen?
Why did you so soon abandon your journey and the freeing of
the Holy Sepulchre? [21] Surely if the word which this base one
reported to us is true, then we and all Christians shall desert you;
neither shall we call you to mind in the future nor even one of
us will dare to invoke Your name." This report of events cast
such a gloomy pall over the army that no one, that is, archbishop,
bishop, abbot, priest, clerk, or any of the laity had the nerve to
invoke the name of Jesus Christ for many days.[22]

No one could console Guy who cried, beat his breast, wrung
his hands, and wailed: "Poor me! Such has happened to Bohemond, the honor and glory of all of the world, the one whom
the universe feared and loved. Alas! Such sadness for me. I am
denied the sight of your most honest face, a sight which I
coveted above all. Would I could die for you, my sweetest
friend and lord? Why was I not stillborn? Why did fate
bring me to this sorrowful day? Why didn't I die in the sea?
Why did I not meet sudden death by falling from a horse and
breaking my neck? I wish that I could have received happy
martyrdom and could have viewed your most glorious death." [23]

---

[20] *Deus verus, trinus et unus* is common. See Blaise, pp. 150, 287, 353, 354;
Troper, p. 61.

[21] The questioning of God's judgment reminds us of Lamentations. The
questioning of God's actions in the crusades became very popular as the
crusading spirit waned. See *Lamentationes Jeremiae* 5:20; Palmer A. Throop,
1940: pp. 68-213.

[22] Tudebode adds archbishop and priest. The *Gesta* does not include these.
See Bréhier, *Gesta*, p. 144.

[23] The lament of Guy is a literary piece, which was copied by later writers.
We cannot believe that a simple knight, who in the words of Sybel was never
carried away by what is strange, wonderful, poetical, or personally interesting,
wrote this. See Heinrich von Sybel, *The History and Literature of the Crusades*,
ed. and trs. Lady Duff Gordon (London, 1861), p. 155. The lament is part of
a tradition based on David's grief over his son, Absalom. David's wish for
death is almost identical with the Tudebode and *Gesta* account. Tudebode and
the *Gesta* wrote *Quis mihi det ut ego moriar pro te.* See Bréhier, *Gesta*, p. 144.
See *Liber secundis Samuelis* 18:33: *Quis mihi tribuat ut ego moriar pro te.*
See Ambrose for a like tradition; *De Excessu fratris sui Satyri, MPL* 16, 1379-
1380. See our *Raymond IV*, p. 85.

Following this outburst, all rushed to him to give comfort so that he would put an end to his laments. Finally Guy composed himself and said: "Perhaps you believe this old disgraceful knight, Stephen. Listen, I have never heard of any of his military exploits. But he has fled basely and disgracefully just as an evil and wretched man. Whatever the wretch says, you will know that it is a lie."

In the meantime Alexius gave the following commands to his troops: "Go and lead all of the people of this land into Bulgaria [24] and carry booty and scorch the earth so that the Turks will find nothing upon their arrival." Reluctantly our people retraced their steps, sorrowing and mourning bitterly even to death. Many pilgrims weakened by disease could not keep pace with the troops and lay dying along the way, while all of the others returned to Constantinople.[25]

During this time, we who were in Antioch had heard the report of Peter Bartholomew, which told how the Apostle Saint Andrew came and showed him the Lance of Jesus Christ and its hiding place. Then Peter came to Raymond of Saint-Gilles and told him to go to the church of Saint Peter where the Lance was hidden. Following this news Raymond joyfully came to the church, and there Peter showed him the place before the door of the choir to the right side. There from morning to evening twelve men dug a deep hole and Peter found the Lance of Jesus Christ, just as Saint Andrew had disclosed, on the fourteenth day of incoming June. They accepted it with great joy, and singing *Te Deum laudamus* they bore it happily to the altar. Thus great euphoria seized the city. Upon report of this discovery, the Frankish army came to Saint Peter's Church to see the Lance. Likewise Greeks, Armenians, and Syrians came singing in high pitch Kyrie eleison and saying: *"Kalo Francia fundari Christo exsi."* [26]

---

[24] Alexius was, if we can believe Anna, frightened. The use of Bulgaria is difficult to explain. See Bréhier, *Gesta*, p. 146, n. 1.

[25] The retreat of Alexius left him open to Bohemond's charge that he violated his pledge of assistance.

[26] The account of Tudebode summarizes that of Raymond d'Aguilers but has some variant material. The *Gesta* likewise follows Raymond's version and uses some of his words. He fails to mention the name of Peter Bartholomew and states that thirteen men (with exception of variants) dug there. The author of the *Gesta* states that he was a witness in the church during the digging. It appears to us that he uses first person here to give credence to his story. His

After these events all the crusaders assembled in a council to decide how to wage battle with the Turks.[27] But first all approved the idea of sending a courier to Kerbogha and God's enemies, the Turks, who would question them as follows: "Why do you enter Christian lands?" So they sent Peter the Hermit and Herluin, an interpreter,[28] and instructed them: "Go to the accursed Turks and wisely converse with them and ask them why they boldly and haughtily entered our Christian lands?" Continue to ask: "Do you know that many of our people wonder why you have come here? We believe, perhaps, that you have come to accept Christianity and that you believe in the one true Lord, born of the Virgin Mary, in whom we believe. If, indeed, you come without this in mind, our leaders, both great and small, beg you to depart hastily from the land of God and the Christians in which the Blessed Apostle Peter a long time ago preached the Gospel and recalled it to the Christian religion, and afterward was elected first bishop.[29] If you follow their requests, the leaders will permit you to depart with all of your possessions; that is, horses, mules, asses, camels, and sheep; and further, they will allow you to take cattle and all other equipment you wish to go from the land." [30]

---

account is short and devoid of detail. It seems that an eyewitness would have known more. See Bréhier, *Gesta*, p. 146. Tudebode relates that after the uncovering of the Lance the crowd came to view the Lance at Saint Peter's church. Tudebode wrote: "Greeks, Armenians, and Syrians came singing in high pitch Kyrie eleison and saying: *'Kalo Francia fundari Christo exsi.'*" This information is not in the *Gesta* or Raymond's book. The Kyrie was subject to additions or farcing. See *Troper* p. xix. There is a suggestion that this Kyrie had an interpolation, part Greek and part Latin following the common idea. Bib. Nat, Paris, MS Latin *5135A* (our MS *A*) has *fundari* and does not translate. MS *C* British Museum *Harley* MS *Latin 3904*, folio 44 B, has *condari* and translates *"Boni sunt Franci qui habent lanceam Christi."* Raymond d'Aguilers, *Liber*, p. 70, has *"Ecce lancea que latus eius aperuit unde tocius mundi salus emanavit."* See *Evangelium Secundum Joannem* 19: 34, 35; *RHC* 3: p. 77, note *b*. The Holy Lance was found on June 14, 1098; *H Chr*. 284.

[27] The *Gesta* leads us to believe that the council was held on June 14 and the mission to Kerbogha dispatched soon afterwards. Tudebode modifies it by writing *postea* which meant that the council was held after the uncovering of the Lance. The Bongars *Gesta*, which closely follows Tudebode, does not have this error. See Bréhier, *Gesta*, p. 148, fn. 1; Hagenmeyer, *Gesta*, p. 363. The embassy was sent on June 27, 1098; *H Chr*. 290.

[28] The idea of Christian lands is based on Peter's claim.

[29] See note 47, chap. III.

[30] The reporting of Peter the Hermit's mission is similar in the *Gesta* and Tudebode, although the word order is different in places. Raymond d'Aguilers has a like report but briefer in form. He indicates that the land was under

Then Kerbogha, commander of the army of the Persian sultan, with all of his emirs was filled with arrogant pride, and replied in an insolent manner: "Indeed, we neither desire nor want your God or your Christianity, and we completely reject you and all of your beliefs. Do you think that we came this far in order to marvel why nobility, great and small, whom you might call to mind, should claim this land, which we with courage snatched from an effeminate people? Now do you wish to hear our reply? Return as rapidly as you can and tell your leaders that if all your forces wish to become Turks and to renounce your God with bowed neck, we shall give them this land and much more; namely, cities, castles, wives, and very great inheritances so that henceforth no one shall remain a footman, but all shall be knights just as we are; and we shall always cherish them in dearest friendship. If they refuse to do so, let them know that all shall be killed or led in chains into everlasting captivity in Corozan to serve us and our descendants for eternity." [31]

Our messengers quickly returned to the Christians and reported all this and how the very cruel people replied to them. In the interim our army, demoralized by fear, was undecided on a course of action. In fact they were on the horns of a dilemma; caught on one side by cruel hunger and on the other paralyzed by fear of the Turks. Nevertheless, the Christians carried out instructions just as the Lord Jesus Christ had commanded them through the priest, Stephen, with three days of fasting and by confessing their sins, by processions from one church to another, by absolution, and by faithfully receiving communion of the body and blood of Christ.[32] They also gave alms to the poor and celebrated masses.

Peter's jurisdiction. The speeches give the narrative color. See Bréhier, *Gesta*, p. 148; Raymond d'Aguilers, pp. 60, 61.

[31] The speech of Kerbogha repeats former material. Porchet was given many promises if he renounced Christianity. Kerbogha was likewise filled with arrogant pride. Pride comes before a downfall. The speech has church expressions—*dilectissimus, sempiterna*. See Blaise, pp. 151, 524.

[32] Tudebode writes after discussing the hunger and fear of the Turks: "Nevertheless Christians carried out instructions (*Tamen*)." The *Gesta* uses *Tandem* and ignores that they were carrying out the instructions of the priest, Stephen. Tudebode has a clearer account at this point. The ceremony took place June 25-27, 1098; *H Chr.* 289. See Bréhier, *Gesta*, p. 150, 151, fn. 2. Hagenmeyer, *Gesta*, p. 368, fn. 1.

Then they drew up six lines inside Antioch. In the first rank
was Hugh the Great with the Franks and the Count of Flanders;
in the second was Duke Godfrey and his army. The Norman
Robert and his men were in the third group. In the fourth was
Adhémar, Bishop of Le Puy, carrying with him the Lance of our
Saviour Jesus Christ, along with his troops and the Provençal
army. Raymond of Saint-Gilles remained behind in Antioch to
guard the mountain because of fear that the defenders of the
citadel would attack the city. In the fifth was Tancred, son of
the marquis, with his troops, accompanied by Gaston of Béarn
with his soldiers and those of the Count of Poitou.[33] In the sixth,
was Bohemond and his crusaders.

Our bishops, priests, clerks, and monks, clad in sacerdotal
garments, marched out of Antioch with the army, carrying
crosses in their hands, praying and begging God that He save
them and guard and deliver them from all peril and evil. Others
stood on the wall by the gate of Antioch, holding sacred crosses
in their hands, making the sign of the Cross, and blessing the
army. Thus arrayed in battle formation and protected by the
sign of the Cross, the crusaders began to march out of Antioch
by the gate which is before *La Mahomerie*.[34]

When Kerbogha saw the Frankish army leave Antioch, one
formation following another in well-executed maneuvers, he
commanded: "Permit them to come out of Antioch so that we
can have a better chance of capturing the main force."[35] The
footmen of Hugh the Great and the Count of Flanders first
marched out, and then each rank followed in its order. Follow-

---

[33] The account of the *Gesta*, Tudebode, and Raymond d'Aguilers are in
agreement on the number of divisions. Only Tudebode mentions Gaston of
Béarn and the soldiers of the Count of Poitou. Tudebode has Gaston to
accompany Tancred. Besly identifies Tudebode with the contingent from
Poitou. Raymond d'Aguilers claims that he carried the Holy Lance. See
Raymond d'Aguilers, pp. 61, 63; Bréhier, *Gesta*, pp. 150, 152.

[34] The description of the roles of the churchmen in Raymond, the *Gesta*,
and Tudebode are so close that it is apparent that there was copying. The
Gesta uses the first person to give authenticity to his version. See Raymond
d'Aguilers, pp. 62, 63; Bréhier, *Gesta*, p. 152.

[35] Raymond d'Aguilers also notes that Kerbogha permitted the crusaders to
march out unmolested. He also adds a conversation of Kerbogha and Mirdalin.
Only Tudebode notes the moving out of the footmen of Hugh the Great and
the Count of Flanders. This is an example in which he has additional information. It is strange that he would have used the word *pedones* (*footmen*), a
so-called southern Italian word, when he was not following the *Gesta*.

ing the emergence of the Christian army from the city, Kerbogha became very apprehensive when he saw the great size of the Frankish forces. Consequently, he instructed the emir who was commander of the field operation that if he saw a signal fire rise in the front ranks that he should immediately sound retreat and withdraw Turkish forces, because he would know that they had lost the day. Kerbogha at once little by little began to retire toward the mountain, only to be followed by our army in like moves.[36]

Then the Turks split their forces; one marched toward the sea while the other kept its position. By this move they hoped to trap our army between the two units. Upon observing the Turkish move, our forces formed a seventh line from the troops of Duke Godfrey and the Count of Normandy and made Count Rainardus commander of it.[37] This unit moved against the Turkish contingents coming from the sea. The Turks then engaged them in battle and inflicted heavy casualties with arrows. Our other group drew up ranks between the river and the mountain, a distance of two miles. The second Turkish force began to advance from their position and to surround our men and to wound them by hurling missiles and shooting arrows.

In addition, a vast army riding white horses and flying white banners rode from the mountains. Our forces were very bewildered by the sight of this army until they realized that it was Christ's aid, just as the priest, Stephen, had predicted. The leaders of this heavenly host were Saint George, the Blessed Demetrius, and the Blessed Theodore.[38] Now this report is credible

[36] The instructions given by Kerbogha are probably literary devices. It is doubtful that the chroniclers had information on Kerbogha's instructions to his men.

[37] Bréhier conjectures that the seventh line shows the wisdom of Bohemond. Raymond d'Aguilers reports no such line. Rainardus, according to William of Tyre, was from Toul. A C manuscript of the Gesta states that he was from Beauvais. See Hagenmeyer, Gesta, p. 373, fn. 21; Bréhier, Gesta, p. 155, fn. 3; La Chanson d'Antioche 2: p. 219 ("Rainars de Tors").

[38] The Gesta does not mention that this was the aid which had been promised by Stephen. Tudebode omits Mercurius and adds Theodore. Mercurius was an Armenian soldier martyred in 259 A.D. There is a Saint Mercurius known for his slaying of Julian. Raymond d'Aguilers has an account of the relics of Saint George and Saint Mercurius. See Raymond d'Aguilers, pp. 111-113; Hagenmeyer, Gesta, p. 375, fn. 28. Bréhier writes of the three as protectors of the Byzantine army. See Bréhier, Gesta, p. 155, fn. 5. The celestial horseback riding is suggested by Prophetia Zachariae 6:1-7 and Apocalypsis B. Joannis Apostoli 6: 1-3; 19:11. See our article, Hill and Hill, 1960: p. 76 for white banners.

because many Christians saw it. The Turkish division flanking
the sea became aware of their inability to endure more and
kindled a grass fire so that the view of it would precipitate the
flight of those in camp. At the sight of the signal fire, the Turks
seized and fled with all of their prized possessions and booty.[39]

Our soldiers gradually fought their way to the Turkish tents
where the greatest resistance lay. Duke Godfrey, the Count of
Flanders, and Hugh the Great rode along the banks of the river,
where the Turkish strength was concentrated. Protected by the
sign of the Cross, this force was the first to launch a coordinated
assault on Kerbogha's troops. After observing this attack, our
other line struck the enemy. The Turks and other pagans then
yelled out; and our men, appealing to the One and True God,
spurred their mounts against the foe. Thus in the name of Jesus
Christ and the Holy Sepulchre they engaged in battle, and with
God's help the Christians overwhelmed the infidels.

The shocked Turks took to flight closely pursued by our men
as far as their tents. Our knights of Christ, more zealous to pur-
sue than search for plunder, chased them as far as the Orontes
bridge and at length to Tancred's castle.[40] The Turks abandoned their tents in addition to gold, silver, many trappings,
sheep, cattle, horses, mules, camels, grain, wine, flour, and an
abundance of other goods necessary to our welfare.[41] The Armenian and Syrian inhabitants of the area, after news of our

---

Raymond d'Aguilers reports a sweet shower from heaven and also a multiplica-
tion of troops. He had reported celestial troops at the battle of Dorylaeum.
See Raymond d'Aguilers, pp. 28, 63. It was customary for a writer to state
that visions were credible because others had seen them. Three witnesses were
necessary according to Raymond d'Aguilers, p. 101.

[39] Raymond d'Aguilers does not indicate that the fire was set as a signal for
retreat. See Raymond d'Aguilers, p. 63.

[40] It is interesting to note that the *Gesta* and Tudebode mention that the
crusaders did not stop to plunder. Peter Bartholomew had so instructed them
according to Raymond d'Aguilers. This is again evidence that they were using
a common source because the *Gesta* and Tudebode do not report Bartholomew's
instructions in detail. They either drew from Raymond d'Aguilers or a source
common to the three writers. There is a question of the extent of the flight.
Bréhier thinks that there was pursuit to the west (Tancred's mountain) and
to the east to the Orontes bridge. See Bréhier, *Gesta*, p. 157, fn. 3, and
Hagenmeyer, *Gesta*, p. 378, fn. 42, for a different opinion. The battle was
fought on June 28, 1098, *H Chr.* 291.

[41] The accounts of the booty in the *Gesta*, Tudebode, and Raymond are
similar. Raymond likens the flight to that of the Syrians at Samaria. See
Raymond d'Aguilers, p. 64.

conquest of the Turks, circled around the mountain to cut them off and killed as many as they could catch.[42] We returned to Antioch joyously, lauding and blessing God, Who bestowed victory upon His people.

The emir, custodian of the citadel, was greatly angered and at the same time frightened when he saw Kerbogha and all of the pagan host abandoning the battlefield before the Frankish army, and in haste he began to seek a Frankish banner. The Count of Saint-Gilles, who stood guard before the citadel, gave orders for his banner to be carried to the emir, who forthwith accepted it gladly, and carefully flew it from the highest tower.[43] Later he sought the banner of Bohemond, who gave it to him after the battle. So the emir received Bohemond's banner with great delight and pleasure. In addition, he made a pact with Bohemond by which those who wished to be Christians could join the Norman's forces, and those who wished to go into Corozan could travel there safe and sound. Bohemond accepted the emir's demands and immediately posted his men in the citadel. Shortly thereafter the emir was baptized along with those who chose to accept Christ; and Bohemond had those who refused to turn apostate to be led into Saracen lands.[44] This battle was fought on the twenty-eighth of June, the vigil of the Apostles Peter and Paul, in the reign of our Lord Jesus Christ, to Whom is the honor and glory throughout eternity. Amen.[45]

[42] The Armenians and Syrians took like action after the defeat of Yaghi Siyan.

[43] Ahmad-ibn-Marwān, custodian of the citadel, opened it to Bohemond, Raymond of Saint-Gilles, the Duke, and the Count of Flanders, according to Raymond d'Aguilers. Tudebode indicates that the emir had agreed to surrender it in case of Kerbogha's defeat. The *Gesta* has an interpolation at this point patently to glorify Bohemond and to add zest to the story. See Raymond d'Aguilers, p. 65; Bréhier, *Gesta*, p. 158.

[44] Raymond d'Aguilers maintains that Bohemond demanded the citadel and the gates. Only Raymond of Saint-Gilles objected. See Raymond d'Aguilers, p. 65.

[45] Raymond d'Aguilers ends his account in a similar style. We think that the ending of chapters with a doxology was not just common to the *Gesta* and Tudebode. In fact the *Gesta* and Tudebode endings are not identical in many places. The doxology is common. See Absolution (Office) Ordinary, II Nocturn; Bréhier, *Gesta*, xi; Raymond d'Aguilers, p. 64.

IX. Sojourn in Antioch and Crusader Raids

AFTER THE DEFEAT all of our enemies, for which we offer deserved praise to God Almighty and the Holy Sepulchre, the Turks scampered away in disarray; some half alive and some wounded took refuge in valleys, groves, and fields. En route they met death because the Greeks, Armenians, and Syrians, after news of the Turkish debacle, lay in ambush killing and wounding them. Our pilgrims returned to Antioch, rejoicing and boasting of their great and successful triumph over the adversaries of God and sacred Christianity.[1]

Then all of our leaders assembled in a council in the church of Saint Peter to decide how to govern and lead the people favorably until they resumed the journey to the Holy Sepulchre, for which many had so faithfully suffered untold hardships. The council, in view of the very arid and parched conditions in summer, resolved not to invade Saracen lands at this time; for they dared not cross that way because they could not lead and protect Christ's people. So they set a time limit as the first of November, the Feast of All Saints, in which all would assemble in Antioch and happily begin the journey to the Holy Sepulchre. All likewise accepted this decision as right and wise.[2]

Subsequently, each one of our leaders departed for his own land, that is into cities and castles until the time of departure

---

[1] Raymond d'Aguilers indicates that the return of the crusaders was a triumph. Tudebode offers thanks to God Almighty and the Holy Sepulchre. The *Gesta* offers thanks to God *trino et uno*. Both Tudebode and the *Gesta* carry out the idea of a Christian triumph. See *Apocalypsis B. Joannis* 19: 6, 7; *Prophetia Sophoniæ* 3: 14-17. Tudebode writes of Greeks, Armenians, and Syrians engaging in the slaughter. The *Gesta* omits this information here. See Raymond d'Aguilers, p. 64; Bréhier, *Gesta*, p. 160.

[2] Tudebode omits the accounts of the sending of Hugh the Great to Constantinople. Raymond d'Aguilers has a like omission. The decision of the council was a wise one but not popular with clerics and pilgrims, who depended more upon God's mercy than upon common sense. Bréhier discusses the weather conditions which influenced the decision. See Bréhier, *Gesta*, p. 162, n. 2. Raymond d'Aguilers reflects the clerical reaction to the decision of the council. See Raymond d'Aguilers, p. 65. The *Gesta* and Raymond set the date for departure as the kalends of November; Tudebode adds Feast of All Saints. He also adds that the council was an amicable one. The conference was held on July 3, 1098; *H Chr.* 298.

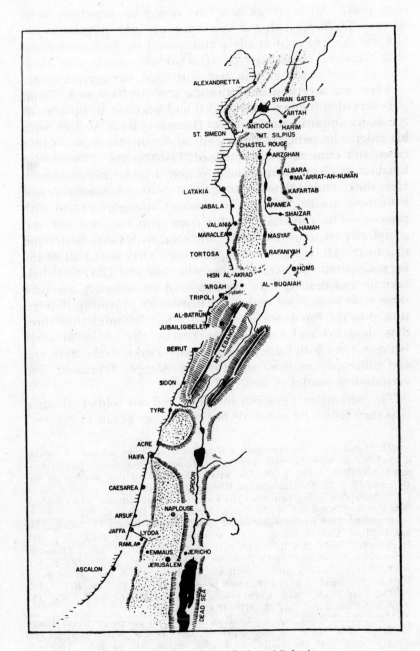

MAP 2. The Crusaders in Syria and Palestine.

drew near.[3] All of the princes gave orders to spread the news throughout Antioch that if by chance any poor pilgrim in the city was short of gold or silver and wished to make a covenant with them, he should not be reluctant to remain with them because they would give in free will what was agreed upon.[4]

There was a certain knight in the army of Raymond, Count of Saint-Gilles, named Raymond Pilet,[5] who had in his entourage many knights and retainers. Departing from Antioch with his troops, he penetrated Saracen lands, by-passed two pagan cities, and came to a castle named Tell-Mannas.[6] The Syrian inhabitants of the town quickly placed it under his command. Here the crusaders dawdled for eight days until messengers came with these words: "Nearby is a Saracen stronghold filled with pagans." The Christian knights thereupon marched out and completely encircled the place, and soon with God's help [7] and that of the Holy Sepulchre captured it. They seized all of the pagans, spared the lives of those who accepted Christ as their Saviour and desired holy baptism, and immediately executed those who would not embrace Christianity. Joyously they returned to the fortification which they had left, and after three days departed and came to the nearby city of Ma'arrat-an-Nu'mān [8] in which were gathered many Turks, Arabs, Saracens, and other pagans from the cities of Aleppo, Damascus, and surrounding castles.

The barbarians came out to battle, and our soldiers thought that they would be attacked; but the enemy began to flee only

---

[3] The *Gesta* states that the princes *divisi sunt* and then set out. Raymond d'Aguilers later uses the term *inter se divisi*. See Bréhier, *Gesta*, p. 162; Raymond d'Aguilers, *Liber*, p. 84. We have a discussion of this problem in our *Raymond IV*, p. 95. See Hagenmeyer, *Gesta*, p. 385, fn. 13.

[4] Tudebode's wording here gives the idea of a feudal contract, an idea which is not so well conveyed in the *Gesta*. See Bréhier, *Gesta*, p. 162.

[5] Raymond Pilet has been identified as a Limousin knight by Bréhier. He was Lord of Alais according to the authors of *HGL*. See *HGL* 3: p. 483. Hagenmeyer thinks that Raymond Pilet set out on July 14, 1098. Runciman believes that he left on July 17, 1098. See Runciman, 1951: p. 251; *H Chr*. 301.

[6] Tell-Mannas was a village southeast of Antioch and near Ma'arrat-an-Nu'mān. Raymond of Saint-Gilles took possession on July 17, 1098; *H Chr*. 302.

[7] The *Gesta* adds, "with Christ's help." See Bréhier, *Gesta*, p. 162. The fortification was seized July 25, 1098; *H Chr*. 306.

[8] Ma'arrat-an-Nu'mān was southeast of Antioch on the route from Hamah to Aleppo. The battle was fought July 27, 1098; *H Chr*. 307. The Gesta errs when it states that the battle was fought on the fifth of July. Tudebode does not make this error. See *Gesta*, p. 164.

to return to fight with our men all day and until sundown. Because of the unbearable heat our forces could not stand the parching dryness, and since they could find no fountains for quenching their thirst, they wished to return safely to their camp. On account of their sins and transgressions [9] the Syrians and the poor, now beset by great thirst and seized by hysteria, withdrew in haste toward their castle. The Turks began to strike fiercely when they saw the Christians in retreat; and it is not astonishing that the victory gave them strength. Many of the crusaders happily surrendered their souls to God for Whose love they had gathered there.[10] Arnold Tudebode, a great knight, was among those killed.[11] At the end of the battle the Christian survivors returned to their castle, where they remained several days.

In the interim the crusaders who remained in Antioch were happy and lighthearted because the bad news had not reached them, and they were ignorant of the fate of their brothers. Their leader and shepherd was Adhémar, Bishop of Le Puy, who by God's will fell mortally ill and by God's nod, resting in peace, fell asleep in the Lord, namely in the bosom of Abraham, Isaac, and Jacob, on the Feast of Saint Peter in Chains.[12] His most happy soul rejoiced with the angels. There was anguish as well as tribulation [13] and untold sorrow in the Christian army because he was a sustainer of the poor and the adviser of the rich. Adhémar also regulated the clergy, preached, and admonished the knights and other well-to-do people, warning them: "Not a one of you can find salvation unless you honor and renew the

[9] "On account of their sins and transgressions"; see The Offertory (Missal, Order of the Mass).

[10] Apparently the pilgrims and the Syrians were responsible for the rout.

[11] Tudebode is the only chronicler to note the death of Arnold Tudebode. It is possible that he was a brother of the author, but Tudebode does not state it. It is strange that such a short notice is given. See Hagenmeyer, *Gesta*, p. 388, 389, fn. 32.

[12] Adhémar died on August 1, 1098; *H Chr.* 308. In the bosom of Abraham, Isaac, and Jacob may be found in the *Missale 1474* I p. 487 (Post Communion). Earlier, Tudebode had Porchet requesting to be carried to the bosom of Abraham. *Evangelium Secundum Lucam* 16:22; *Sarum Missal*, ed. Legg, 1916: p. 434. The addition of Isaac and Jacob shows the influence of liturgy. The *Gesta* does not include this material. The description of Adhémar's death (Asleep in the Lord) is ecclesiastical. See *Epistola B. Pauli Apostoli ad Corinthios Prima* 15:16-18.

[13] Anguish and tribulation (*angustia et tribulatio.*) See *Epistola B. Pauli ad Romanos* 2:9; *Prophetia Isaiae* 30:6.

strength of the poor clerks. You cannot be redeemed without them, and they cannot live without you. It behooves them daily to offer prayers to God for your transgressions in which you have offended in many unforgivable ways, and you should rule and feed the poor since they do not have the wisdom to seek and to find as do you. Therefore, I ask you to cherish them for the love of God and sustain them with all of your resources." [14]

Shortly after this the venerable Raymond, Count of Saint-Gilles, moved into Saracen lands and came to a town named Albara, which he besieged with his army.[15] By God's will he captured it in a short time and then killed all the Saracens, males and females, noble and lesser folk, whom he could find there. Following his establishment of authority, Raymond returned Albara to the Christian faith; and he began without delay to seek along with his wisest advisers how he could faithfully choose a most devoted bishop in Albara who would return the city to God's care, and deliver it from the devil's house to the living and true God, and dedicate there the oratories of the saints to the pure in heart. Afterwards he chose a certain clerk whom he conducted to Antioch for consecration. Following these ceremonies, the new bishop held councils as a replacement for Adhémar, Bishop of Le Puy.[16]

As the date of departure, that is the Feast of All Saints, drew close, all of our leaders came back to Antioch with the exception of Bohemond, who was in parts of Romania seized by a grave illness.[17] For that reason the departure date was delayed.

[14] The preaching of Adhémar is probably an interpolation drawn from the homilies. Raymond d'Aguilers has similar instructions for feeding the poor when Adhémar and Saint Andrew appear to Peter Bartholomew in a vision. See Raymond d'Aguilers, p. 69.

[15] Albara (al-Barāh) was located forty-two miles southeast of Antioch. Raymond's movements are poorly defined. He did not set out before September 1, 1098. He probably operated out of Chastel-Rouge and captured Albara about September 25, 1098; H Chr. 316.

[16] Peter of Narbonne was a priest in Raymond's army. This is the first move to establish a Latin hierarchy in the Near East. However, the Greek patriarch, John, consecrated Peter as Bishop of Albara. The Gesta and Tudebode parallel at this point. See Bréhier, Gesta, pp. 166, 168. The devil's house; see Apocalypsis B. Joannis 2:9. The oracula sanctorum comes to mean in mediaeval Latin a place of prayer. See Liber Leviticus 16:2; The living and true God; see Epistola B. Pauli Apostoli ad Thessalonicenses Prima 1:9.

[17] The Gesta and Raymond d'Aguilers ignore the fact that Bohemond was late because of illness. The Feast of All Saints is on November 1. Bohemond returned on November 3, 1098; H. Chr. 322.

Then the time came when he could fight, so Bohemond came at once to Antioch, where the others were assembled. Thereafter all of the lords came together in a council and began to seek means by which they could resume the march to the Holy Sepulchre saying: "Since the time is opportune and very favorable, why delay longer?" [18]

But Bohemond daily sought the implementation of the convention; namely, the returning of Antioch to him, which the other leaders had confirmed. He complained bitterly concerning Raymond, Count of Saint-Gilles, since he would have no part of the convention which Bohemond sought because the count feared to perjure himself with the emperor. Afterward they met frequently in the church of Saint Peter, in the course of which meetings Bohemond repeated terms of the agreement to the audience, and Raymond narrated his words and oath which he had sworn to Alexius on the counsel of Bohemond.[19]

The bishops, Duke Godfrey, Count Robert of Flanders, Robert of Normandy, Count Eustace, and other leaders withdrew from the others and entered the church by the chair of Saint Peter, so that within the church they could pronounce judgment on the contentions of Bohemond and Raymond.[20] But fearful that the journey to the Holy Sepulchre would not be resumed, they equivocated. When Raymond of Saint-Gilles became aware of this problem, he offered: "Rather than give up the journey to the Holy Sepulchre, if Bohemond shall choose to come with us, I shall carry out willingly whatever the bishops, Duke Godfrey, Robert the Norman, Count Robert of Flanders, and the

---

[18] Tudebode writes that the council said: "Since the time is opportune and very favorable why delay longer." The *Gesta* writes "It is not the time for quarreling more." See Bréhier, *Gesta,* p. 168. It seems to us that the author of the *Gesta* was writing after the event as was Raymond d'Aguilers and that the quarrel became more bitter a few weeks after this meeting. Raymond d'Aguilers wrote of a peace of discord. See Raymond d'Aguilers, pp. 74, 75.

[19] It is interesting to note that the *Gesta* and Tudebode write of Raymond taking the oath to Alexius on the advice of Bohemond. See Bréhier, *Gesta,* p. 169, fn. 6, for Bréhier's opinion that the Count of Saint-Gilles became sympathetic to Alexius to block Bohemond. We do not agree with this view. We think that Raymond had a consistent policy of friendship with Alexius. See John Hugh Hill, 1951.

[20] The *Gesta* and Raymond d'Aguilers do not mention the presence of Count Eustace. The crusaders met in the choir of the cathedral, probably on November 5, 1098, to November 18, 1098; *H Chr.* 323.

other princes recommend, if it does not interfere with my
fidelity to Alexius."

Bohemond praised the proposal and agreed to it. Thus they
promised, by joining hands with the bishops [21] in the presence
of the pilgrims, that in no circumstances would the march to the
Holy Sepulchre be abandoned. Bohemond subsequently con-
sulted with his men on means by which he could fortify the citadel on the heights of the mountain with arms and food adequate
for a protracted stay.[22] In turn, Raymond of Saint-Gilles fortified the palace of Yaghi Siyan and the tower which is above the
Bridge Gate in the sector adjacent to Port Saint Simeon.[23]

Antioch is a very important, beautiful, and noted city, within
whose walls are four very large and lofty mountains.[24] Crowning
the highest mountain is the very strong and tall citadel. The
famous and agreeable city lies below. It is aesthetically designed,
since inside the town there are most beautiful waters which flow
through fountains from the mountains. There are twelve hundred churches, three hundred and sixty monasteries with monks,
as well as a patriarch who governs one hundred and fifty-three
bishops. Antioch is enclosed by two walls, the most important
of which is very tall, constructed of large stones, and on which
are arranged four hundred and fifty towers. In short, Antioch
is superbly planned. On the east it is hemmed in by four towering mountains, and on the west following the walls of the city
the great river, the Orontes, flows. Because it is so desirable and
beautiful, no one wished to be foolish enough to abandon this

---

[21] The *Gesta* notes the presence of bishops there. Raymond d'Aguilers
makes the quarrel appear more serious. He also reveals that the people put
pressure on Raymond and Bohemond. See Raymond d'Aguilers, p. 75; Bréhier,
Gesta, p. 168.

[22] The "peace of discord" was, no doubt, favorable to Bohemond, who apparently had no intention of leaving Antioch.

[23] Raymond of Saint-Gilles fortified the palace of Yaghi Siyan and the gate
near *La Mahomerie*. Bohemond with command of the citadel possessed an
advantage. He also did not have to worry about his image with the pilgrims.

[24] Bréhier prefers to place the description of Antioch in an appendix and
treat it as an interpolation. Hagenmeyer in following Bongars' work, which
more nearly parallels Tudebode here, includes it as does Tudebode. The
description of cities and Holy Places was a part of historical writing. Raymond
has a description of Antioch at the very opening of the siege. See Raymond
d'Aguilers, pp. 30, 31. Saint Ambrose has a description of Antioch, which
may have been somewhat of a pattern. See Ambrose, *De Excidio Urbis
Hierosolimitanae*, MPL 15: 2175.

regal city of Antioch.[25] It was of such great power that seventy-five kings formerly ruled there. The names of these kings were: [26]

Mirgulandus, Ebramdons, Lamuirafres, Rademons, Helias, Calarfines, Brumandus, Margories, Faraon, Brumandus, Prelion, Laidus, Rudandus, Iudas Machabeus, Nubles, Samson, David Hereticus, Salomon, Pilatus, Herodes, Helidius, Gafernus, Rudandus, Galderius, Morfirius, Fortis Eustras, Maraon, Argolas, Ordotius, Fortis Lamusteoc, Alapres Amiralius, Morabilis, Orgidandum, Morlionus, Organnus, Gorbandus Impius de Samarzana, Bracerandus, Morus Rex, Pulcher Clarandus, Ariandon, Rex Thanas, Escomus, Duras, Dromandus, Rex Vision, Satanus, Tobus, Lintion, Malardus, Dairamornus, Mordandus, Drahonus, Brumories, Apparandus, Effremion, Noirandus, Fortis Bruas, Corgandus, Udonus, Impius Telandus, Pelufres, Troandus, Candelos Rex, Rambulandus, Gazani, Mirmon, Oringes, Brulion, Mardrolienus, Droliandus, Daribonus, Ga-

---

[25] Tudebode is a bit more descriptive than the *Gesta*. He writes of fountains and twelve hundred churches. See Bréhier, *Gesta*, p. 221, append. fn. 4, for the number of monasteries and bishops. Justinian fortified Antioch after a Persian attack. Raymond wrote: "It may dread neither the attack of machine nor the assault of man." See Raymond d'Aguilers, pp. 30, 31. See Downey for a discussion of the choice of site, water supplies, disadvantage of Mount Silpius, and the controlling citadel; Downey, 1961: pp. 63, 65. See his description of churches and monasteries in and near Antioch, pp. 612, 621. He also describes the activities of Peter in Antioch, pp. 582, 586.

[26] The *Gesta* writes that there were seventy-five kings, the first of whom was Antiochus, but the author does not include the list, which is given by Tudebode. Tudebode's catalog of kings is interesting in that it notes a list of Saracen names available to writers anterior to the *Chansons de Geste* in their present form. The Bréhier *Gesta* cites the existence of such a list but does not quote. See Bréhier, *Gesta*, p. 222, fn. 1. Albert of Aachen cites a group, calling them Turkish leaders. See Albert, p. 394; *La Chanson d'Antioche* 2: p. 260, gives a list. Ernest Langlois finds many Saracen names recurring in two or more epics as do we. See Langlois, 1904. The following examples will illustrate: *Alapres Amiralius* (Tudebode); *Brodoam de Alapia* or *Halapia* (Albert, p. 394); *Antiochus* (Tudebode); *Antiochus* (*La Chanson d'Antioche* 2: p. 260) and Langlois, *op. cit.*, p. 38; *Nubles* (Tudebode); *de Nubles* (*La Chanson de Roland*, ed. and tr. Gautier, 1887: p. 290, line 3224); *Roi de Nubie* (*La Conquête de Jerusalem*, ed. Hippeau, 1868: p. 157).

The endings of Tudebode's names suggest their occurrence in verse, where such names were particularly useful to fill out lines or as a catalog to expand the story. The most popular ending in Tudebode's list was *-us* followed next in descending order by *-andus*. It is interesting to note that Eginhard's name for Roland was Hruodlandus. See Eginhard, *Vie de Charlemagne*, ed. and tr. Louis Halphen, 1923: p. 13.

zianus, Bromirius, and Antiochus who was the chief of all of these, and from him the city of Antioch is named.[27]

The pilgrims to the Holy Sepulchre, as you have heard before, besieged Antioch for eight months and one day.[28] Soon afterward they were besieged in Antioch by the Turks and other pagans for twenty-six days.[29] Then with the aid of God and the Holy Sepulchre the pilgrims rested happily and joyously in Antioch for five and one-half months.[30]

On the eighth day before the end of the month of November, Raymond of Saint-Gilles, attended by his army, left Antioch and came to a city called Rugia and from there marched to Albara. On the fourth day before the end of November, he arrived before Ma'arrat-an-Nu'mān, a town swarming with Saracens, Turks, Arabs, and many other pagans.[31] On the following day Raymond and his forces launched an attack on the town, but he could not take it because the will of the Lord had not so decreed. Close on Raymond's heels, Bohemond and his army arrived and encamped around Ma'arrat-an-Nu'mān on the Lord's day.[32] On Monday they made such a staunch attack on all sides against the city that they pushed scaling ladders against the walls. In the melee the crusaders struck with lances and swords, but

[27] Tudebode ends the list by stating that Antiochus was the chief of these kings. Certainly many conjectures have been made on the merits of Tudebode's work. In his case we can conjecture that the author of the Gesta omitted Tudebode's list or that Tudebode added to the Gesta. It is a good example of the hazards of arguing from silence.

[28] Tudebode uses a phrase, "as you have heard before," which makes his account more sensible than that of Gesta. Tudebode informs his reader that he is summarizing. The Gesta account dangles. Bréhier, who created a text according to his notion, places this dating in the appendix, where it makes no sense. See Bréhier, Gesta, p. 223, fn. 3, 4; Hagenmeyer, Gesta, p. 400, fn. 16.

[29] The Gesta states that they were besieged three weeks. See Bréhier, Gesta, p. 222; Tudebode writes that they were besieged twenty-six days.

[30] The Gesta states five months and eight days. See Bréhier, Gesta, p. 222. Tudebode writes five months and a half.

[31] Raymond of Saint-Gilles was accompanied by Robert of Flanders. See Raymond d'Aguilers, p. 75. The crusaders left Antioch on November 23, 1098, and arrived at Ma'arrat-an-Nu'mān on November 27, 1098, and attacked the town the next day; H Chr. 324, 325, 326.

[32] Tudebode and the Gesta do not note the presence of other princes. See Bréhier, Gesta, p. 173, fn. 5. However, the Gesta has Bohemond trailing Raymond and participating from the beginning of the siege. Tudebode also has Bohemond following closely after Raymond and joining in an attack on Monday. We do know that Raymond d'Aguilers belabored Bohemond for half-hearted efforts in the siege. See Raymond d'Aguilers, p. 79.

the strength of the pagans was so great on that day that the Christians could harm them in no way but in turn suffered many evils.

Food was scarce because the Christians dared not go anywhere, since the environs were patrolled by a multitude of pagans. The foresighted Blessed Andrew, who never slept but was ever watchful of Christian fears, made known to Peter Bartholomew that if the crusaders would turn from evil and collectively have faith in the good of others, then Peter should instruct them by saying: "Love your brothers as you love yourself; and return that part which He retained when He created this world and all the creatures within; namely, one-tenth of all things which are possessed. He shall give to the Christians Ma'arrat-an-Nu'mān in a short time and fulfill all your wishes. He orders the previously named tithe to be divided into four parts: one of which shall be given to the bishop, one to the priests, one to the churches, and one to the poor." [33] All agreed to this proposition in council.

Soon after Raymond of Saint-Gilles had a very sturdy and tall wooden tower constructed, so that it was designed and built on four wheels. Many knights stood on top of the tower, while Ebradus the Hunter blew loudly on his trumpet as graceful banners waved in front of him; truly it was a beautiful sight.[34] In the lower part of the tower there were more than one hundred armed knights, who rolled it near the city next to a certain tower.[35] The sight of this caused the enemy to build many machines from which they hurled huge stones upon our tower so that they killed almost all of our knights.[36] They shredded the banners which flew on top with arrows and rocks, and rained

[33] Tudebode summarizes a vision of Peter Bartholomew reported by Raymond d'Aguilers. According to Raymond, Peter Bartholomew was visited by Saint Peter and Saint Andrew. See Raymond d'Aguilers, pp. 76-78. Tudebode's version is somewhat different from that of Raymond d'Aguilers and does not reflect slavish copying.

[34] Tudebode writes of the waving of banners, a beautiful sight. This touch of realism, not repeated in the *Gesta*, leads us to believe that Tudebode was an eyewitness. See Bréhier, *Gesta*, p. 172.

[35] Tudebode has one hundred knights in the tower. The *Gesta* gives no such number. See Bréhier, *Gesta*, p. 172.

[36] The machines were ballistae (rock hurlers).

down Greek fire with the expectation of burning the tower.[37] But the good and merciful God did not permit the tower to burn, and it continued to rise above all of the walls and towers of Ma'arrat-an-Nu'mān. In fact, William of Montpellier [38] and many other knights who were on the highest parapet hurled large stones upon the Saracens who manned the wall. Often the stones struck upon shields so shield and pagan tumbled, and the unfortunate one fell to his death. Others held pennoned spears and so with lances and iron hooks tried to drag the enemy in to them.[39] Knights and their retainers battled, while priests and clerks dressed in sacred garments stood behind the tower praying and imploring our Lord Jesus Christ to protect His people, give victory to the knights of Christ, glorify sacred Christianity, and destroy heathenism. Thus they fought until sundown.[40]

Then a most noble knight, Gouffier, first climbed up a ladder which was mounted against the wall.[41] However the ladder soon broke under the weight of a great number of those who followed. But Gouffier, along with others who had reached the top

---

[37] The *Gesta* has no mention of the banners being shredded by arrows and rocks. Again Tudebode gives realism to his account. The Turks apparently had knowledge of the use of Greek fire which had been a closely guarded secret in the Byzantine world. See Bréhier, *Gesta*, p. 174.

[38] William of Montpellier. See note 16, chap. V.

[39] The *Gesta* uses *honorabilia signa*. See Bréhier, *Gesta*, p. 174. Tudebode uses *in astis vexilla*. They were pennons or gonfanons.

[40] Tudebode has a few differences from the *Gesta* at this point. Raymond d'Aguilers omits the clerical activities here. It is a strange omission in view of Raymond's love of clerical participation. However, Raymond does go into lengthy detail of such activities at the time of the defeat of Kerbogha. Tudebode and the *Gesta* have almost an identical passage attached to the battle of Ma'arrat-an-Nu'mān. Tudebode writes of Ma'arrat-an-Nu'mān: "*Obsecrantes dominum nostrum Ihesum Christum ut suum defendebat populum.*" The *Gesta*, likewise reporting on events at Ma'arrat-an-Nu'mān: "*Obsecrantes Deum ut suum defenderet populum.*" Raymond d'Aguilers in reporting events at the time of Kerbogha's defeat wrote: "*Deum invocantes ut populum suum defenderet.*" See *Liber*, p. 81. Note how close the wording of the *Gesta* and Raymond are at this point. Again we cannot understand how Hagenmeyer and Sybel were so sure that the *Gesta* did not copy Raymond in places or a source common to them.

[41] Gouffier of Lastours was lord of Lastours near Nexon (Haute-Vienne). See *Notitiae duae Lemovicenses*, p. 351; see L'Abbé Arbellot, 1881: p. 10, 11. Arbellot repeats a very interesting story of the lion which became a pet of Gouffier and finally drowned when he could not return on a homeward bound ship.

of the wall, began to fight with deadly lances. Other Christians found another ladder and hastily raised it against the wall; and so many knights and footmen mounted and climbed it in such numbers that the wall could scarcely hold them. Then the Saracens rushed upon the crusaders so forcibly from the wall and ground, shooting arrows and engaging them in hand-to-hand combat with spears, that many Christians became hysterical and leaped from the walls. Some very courageous men continued under great pressure to man the walls against the assault, while others under the tower were sapping the wall. The sight of the undermining of the wall terrified the Saracens, who fled pell-mell into the city. These events took place on the Sabbath at the hour of vespers as the sun set on the eleventh day of the incoming December.[42]

Bohemond sent word through an interpreter to the leaders that if they, along with their wives and children, would take their possessions and go to a palace situated above the gate, he would protect their lives. All of our forces broke into Ma'arrat-an-Nu'mān, and each one took as his own property whatever booty he could find in houses and cellars. When day dawned they slew on the spot all Saracen males and females whom they could find. Not one nook of the city was free of Saracen corpses, and a person could hardly walk the streets without stepping on dead bodies. Bohemond seized those whom he had commanded to enter the palace and robbed them of all of their possessions, gold, silver, and other goods. Some he killed; others he ordered to be led away for sale in the slave market of Antioch.[43]

Many of our people in Ma'arrat-an-Nu'mān commandeered the necessities, but many found nothing in the way of booty. Afterward there was such a delay in the city that many were pressed because they did not dare go any distance into Saracen

[42] The capture of Ma'arrat-an-Nu'mān took place on December 11, 1098; *H Chr.* 329.

[43] The role of Bohemond does not put him in a good light. This is in contrast with his treatment of the garrison of the citadel and Bohemond's restraint in attacking Greek towns. For some reason the bright image of Bohemond seems to disappear after the capture of Antioch. If there was a revision of the *Gesta* later, as some critics think, the copyist did not bother about this incident. Raymond d'Aguilers indicates that the knights under Bohemond seized the greatest amount of booty. See Raymond d'Aguilers, p. 79.

lands, and they could find no booty nearby. As a result the Christians of this land brought back nothing for sale. Consequently, our poor people began to split open the pagan corpses because they found bezants hidden in their bellies. There were others who were so famished that they cut the flesh of the dead into bits, cooked, and ate it. When the leaders observed this, they ordered the corpses of the pagans dragged out of the gates of the city, piled into heaps, and afterward they ordered them burned.[44]

Bohemond, unable to agree with Raymond of Saint-Gilles, returned to Antioch. Shortly thereafter Raymond sent couriers to Duke Godfrey, the Count of Flanders, Robert of Normandy, and Bohemond with an invitation to come to Chastel-Rouge for a parley with him. All of the chieftains came and discussed means by which they could resume the journey to the Holy Sepulchre, whose recovery had motivated them and brought them this far.[45] An impasse developed with Bohemond demanding Antioch and Raymond refusing because of the oath which he had taken to Alexius. Consequently, Duke Godfrey and the other counts went back to Antioch. Raymond, that athlete of Christ, returned to Ma'arrat-an-Nu'mān, where the pilgrims to the Holy Sepulchre were encamped. He also sent his men to Antioch with instructions to fortify and guard the palace of Yaghi Siyan, which he had in his power, which is above the Bridge Gate opopsite *La Mahomerie*.

In Ma'arrat-an-Nu'mān the wise Bishop of Orange died,[46] and the pilgrims tarried there for one month and three days. Bohemond in the meantime, desiring to have the city of Antioch in his power, drove out all of the men of Raymond of Saint-Gilles. When the Christian athlete, Raymond, received news of this, he

[44] Tudebode informs us that the corpses of the Saracens were dragged out of the city and burned. The *Gesta* does not give this information. Raymond d'Aguilers states that the bodies of the enemy were thrown into swamps. The three accounts agree on cannibalism. See Bréhier, *Gesta*, pp. 176, 178; Raymond d'Aguilers, p. 81.

[45] The meeting at Chastel-Rouge was probably held on January 4, 1099; *H Chr.* 335. See Raymond d'Aguilers, p. 80, fn. 11.

[46] This was William, Bishop of Orange, who was in the Provençal entourage. He was respected and apparently replaced Adhémar in leadership, although he did not gain his fame. He died at Ma'arrat-an-Nu'mān on December 20, 1098, and was probably buried in the basilica of Saint Andrew; *H Chr.* 332.

regarded it lightly, and as a servant of our Lord Jesus Christ resumed the way to the Holy Sepulchre.[47]

[47] The *Gesta* does not mention Bohemond's ejection of Raymond's troops from Antioch. Raymond d'Aguilers only mentions it casually at the siege of ʿArqah and indicates that Bohemond did so after Raymond's departure. See Raymond d'Aguilers, p. 105. The *Gesta* pretends that Raymond left when he saw that no leaders wished to continue the journey. See Bréhier, *Gesta*, p. 180. Tudebode indicates that Bohemond drove Raymond's men from Antioch before the Count of Saint-Gilles resumed the march and that Raymond took the loss lightly. In view of the later gathering of the leaders, it appears that plans to depart had already been made and that Raymond did not simply depart barefooted with a handful of men. So in the light of later events, Tudebode is more trustworthy here than Raymond d'Aguilers or the *Gesta*. See our *Raymond IV*, p. 114. We think that modern historians have placed undue importance on the quarrels of Raymond and Bohemond. Raymond raided in nearby lands on January 8, 1099, and marched out of Maʿarrat-an-Nuʿmān on January 13, 1099; *H Chr.* 338, 339.

X. The March from Ma'arrat-an-Nu'mān to Jerusalem

SO ON THE THIRTEENTH DAY of incoming January, Raymond of Saint-Gilles marched out of Ma'arrat-an-Nu'mān, barefooted, and arrived at Kafartāb some eight miles distant and remained there for three days to be joined by Robert of Normandy.[1] The king of Shaizar had often sent his couriers to Raymond of Saint-Gilles both while he was at Ma'arrat-an-Nu'mān and in Kafartāb. They carried word that their king wished to accord with Raymond and to give as much from his revenue as the count demanded. Further, the emissaries said the king of Shaizar desired to be diligent in helping the Christians, and he pledged to make pilgrims secure and free of fear so far as his jurisdiction permitted. He also offered to furnish a market in horses and food. As a result the pilgrims moved out and pitched their tents along the Orontes near Shaizar.[2]

Afterward when the king of Shaizar saw the Frankish army in the proximity of the city, he was greatly perturbed and threatened to deny the crusaders a market unless they moved on. However, on the following day he sent two Turkish guides to take them to a ford and to direct them to a likely place for booty. Finally, they entered a valley with a protecting castle and there found more than five thousand animals, adequate amounts of grain, and other provisions, which revived the entire Christian

---

[1] Raymond's resumption of the march in bare feet interested all three of the chroniclers. This act signified the fact that Raymond was considered as a pilgrim. See our book, *Raymond IV*, p. 155. Raymond d'Aguilers states that Tancred, along with forty knights, marched with the Count of Saint-Gilles. See Raymond d'Aguilers, p. 83. Kafartāb was Capharda to the chroniclers. Raymond d'Aguilers does not mention the arrival of Robert of Normandy. Raymond arrived at Kafartāb on January 13, 1099, and was joined by Robert of Normandy probably on January 14, 1099; *H Chr.* 339, 340.

[2] Raymond d'Aguilers confirms the fact that nearby rulers sent messages to Raymond of Saint-Gilles. He also implies that the ruler of Shaizar tricked the crusaders. Shaizar, south of Ma'arrat-an-Nu'mān was ruled by 'Izz al-Dīn Abu'l Asâkir, Sultan of the Banū-Munqidh dynasty. See Grousset, 1934: 1: p. 126; Raymond d'Aguilers, pp. 83, 87. The crusaders arrived at Shaizar on January 16, 1099; *H Chr.* 341.

army.[3] The lord of the castle made an agreement with Raymond, furnished him horses and other supplies, and swore by his law that he would no longer harm the pilgrims. Raymond and his troops delayed there for five days. Following their departure, the Christian pilgrims came to another Arab castle whose lord likewise made an agreement with the Count of Saint-Gilles.[4]

Marching from this place they came to Rafanīyah, a most beautiful city situated in a valley and supplied with all necessities. When word of the approach of the Christian pilgrims spread, the inhabitants abandoned the city along with its gardens filled with vegetables and houses full of edibles.[5] On the third day the Christians left Rafanīyah, passed over a tall and boundless mountain, and descended into the valley of Sem, where there was an abundant supply of grain and cattle.[6] The crusaders remained in the vicinity for fifteen days. Here stood an empty castle, which the inhabitants had put to the torch and then fled.[7] Nearby was another castle which housed a host of pagans.[8] Our pilgrims made such a vicious attack that the castle would have capitulated had not the Saracens stampeded great herds of cattle outside of the walls. So our crusaders returned to their tents with a great number of animals.

At daylight the Christians broke camp and arrived before the afore-mentioned fortification with the intention of pitching their tents and laying siege to it. But the pagan race had van-

[3] Hagenmeyer thinks that the valley of the Orontes was between Shaizar and Hamāh. See Hagenmeyer, *Gesta*, p. 417, fn. 27. The crusaders remained there from January 17 to January 22, 1099; *H Chr.* 342, 343.

[4] Hagenmeyer identifies this castle as Massiyas (Masyāf). See Hagenmeyer, *Gesta*, p. 418, fn. 29.

[5] The crusaders arrived at Rafanīyah (Kephalia in *Gesta*) on January 23, 1099, and left on January 25, 1099; *H Chr.* 344, 345.

[6] The valley of the Sem has been identified as the Buqai'ah valley. The crusaders arrived there on January 27, 1099, *H Chr.* 345. They remained in this area until February 14, 1099. See Bréhier, *Gesta*, p. 183, fns. 3, 4. Raymond d'Aguilers describes the dissension over the route to be taken. See our *Raymond IV*, p. 114, and Raymond d'Aguilers, p. 84.

[7] The *Gesta* does not mention this castle.

[8] Tudebode refers to Krak des Chevaliers or Ḥiṣn al-Akrād. See Dussaud, 1927: p. 92; Deschamps, 1934: pp. 113-115. Raymond d'Aguilers gives a brief description. See Raymond d'Aguilers, p. 86. The castle was defended by Kurds. See Hagenmeyer, *Gesta*, p. 419, fn. 36. The castle controlled routes from Homs and Hamāh to Tripoli. It was occupied on January 29, 1099; *H Chr.* 347.

ished during the night and abandoned their fort to the pilgrims of the Holy Sepulchre. Upon entering the castle, the pilgrims found an abundance of heavenly dew; that is, grain, wine, flour, oil, chickens, and whatever was beneficial to them. They most devoutly celebrated the Feast of the Purification of the Virgin Mary on the second day of February at that place.[9]

Messengers from the city of Camela [10] came there bringing with them horses and gold, which the king of that city sent to Raymond of Saint-Gilles; and they also stated that their ruler wished to make an accord with the count, promising to respect the wishes of the Christians in all things and to honor them in his land. The king of Tripoli also sent his couriers to Raymond of Saint-Gilles, seeking to make peace if it pleased him and, in addition, sent ten horses and four mules as well as bezants.[11] But Raymond would under no consideration entertain peace proposals unless the king embraced Christianity. The king so promised.

After our departure from this fertile valley, the Christians came to the castle named 'Arqah.[12] Here they set up camp on Monday the second day of the week in the middle of February. A great number of pagans, Turks, Saracens, Arabs, Paulicians, and others filled the castle, which they had skillfully fortified and now courageously defended. The castle was very formidable and high, perched upon a mountain and enclosed by two walls.[13] One day fourteen of our knights left the siege and rode to Tripoli, which lay eight miles away. In this reconnoitering

---

[9] The parallels of Tudebode and the *Gesta* are interesting at this point. Tudebode writes of heavenly dew. The *Gesta* does not do so. Tudebode writes "de rore caeli habundantiam licit frumentum, vinuum. . . ." The *Gesta* writes "omnen abundantiam frumenti, vini. . . ." See Bréhier, *Gesta,* p. 182. Genesis writes "Det tibi Deus de rore caeli et de pinguedine terrae, abundantiam frumenti et vini." See *Liber Genesis* 27: 28. The *Gesta* fails to note the loot included chickens.

[10] Camela (ancient Emesa) was Homs. See Bréhier, *Gesta,* p. 183, fn. 7; Hagenmeyer, *Gesta,* p. 422, fn. 43. The date was February 4, 1099; *H Chr.* 350.

[11] Tripoli (Tripolis, Tarābulus) was a port town at the foot of the Lebanon mountains. The emir was Jalāl al-Mulk Abu'l Hassan ibn-'Ammār. Raymond d'Aguilers has a similar account. See Raymond d'Aguilers, p. 87.

[12] 'Arqah ('Irqah, Arca) controlled the routes to Tripoli, Latakia, and Homs. Raymond's siege of it opened him to criticism. See our *Raymond IV,* pp. 121-126. Raymond arrived before 'Arqah on February 14, 1099; *H Chr.* 352.

[13] Tudebode gives a short description of 'Arqah. The *Gesta* and Raymond d'Aguilers do not do so and are similar in their statements concerning the strength of 'Arqah.

force were Viscount Raymond of Turenne, Viscount Peter of
Castillon, Aimericus of Lobenes, Sichardus and Bego of Ribeira,
William Botinus, and others whose names I do not know.[14] The
fourteen Christian knights came upon sixty Turks, Saracens, and
Kurds, who drove before them more than fifteen hundred animals. Strengthened by the sign of the Cross, our men charged
and, with God's help, whipped them, killing six of their number,
and seizing six horses.

On another day Raymond Pilet and Viscount Raymond of
Turenne, accompanied by their knights, arrived before Tortosa
and launched a heavy attack against the town, which was heavily
guarded by a host of infidels. At nightfall our troops fell back
to a secluded nook in the woods, made camp, and lighted many
fires to simulate a large Christian army. The subterfuge struck
terror into the hearts of the defenders, who scampered away in
the dark and left Tortosa [15] with its plentiful supply of goods and
its excellent harbor to the crusaders. On the next day our
knights arrived with plans for attack only to find a ghost town.
They then occupied it for the duration of the siege of ʻArqah.
The ruling emir of the nearby city of Maraclea made a pact with
us and agreed to permit our men within the walls and to fly our
banner.[16]

The other lords who had remained in Antioch, namely Duke
Godfrey, Count Robert of Flanders, and Bohemond came as far
as Latakia in the wake of Raymond of Saint-Gilles.[17] There
Bohemond bid them farewell and returned to Antioch.[18] Duke
Godfrey and the Count of Flanders continued to follow Count
Raymond and came to the city of Gibellum, which they besieged
and attacked vigorously.[19]

[14] See note 41, chap. III, for identification of Peter of Castillon. Raymond
of Turenne was Viscount of Turenne in Limousin. See Arbellot, 1881: p. 43,
and *RHC Occ.* 5: p. 351. The names of the other knights have not been well
identified. See Hagenmeyer, *Gesta*, p. 426, fn. 54. The raid was made on
February 16, 1099; *H Chr.* 353.

[15] Tortosa (Antaradus) was a port city of Syria. Raymond d'Aguilers writes
of its strong fortifications but does not give details of its capture. See Raymond
d'Aguilers, p. 88. Tortosa fell on February 17, 1099; *H Chr.* 354.

[16] Maraclea (Maraqīyah) was a port north of Tortosa.

[17] Latakia (Laodicea, al-Lādhiqīyah) was a port city north of Maraclea.

[18] The crusaders arrived at Latakia toward the end of February, 1099; *H Chr.*
356. Albert of Aachen indicates that Bohemond returned because he coveted
Antioch. See Albert, p. 453.

[19] Gibellum (Gabala, Jabalah) was a small port city between Latakia and
Tortosa. The crusaders besieged it around March 1, 1099; *H Chr.* 357.

In the meantime messengers came to Raymond at the siege of 'Arqah announcing that an approaching force of infidels wished to engage him in battle. Subsequently, he sent the Bishop of Albara to Duke Godfrey and Count Robert of Flanders with instructions for them to come to 'Arqah, because the pagans were assembled on all sides ready to do battle with him and his troops. After this news Duke Godfrey and the Count of Flanders made an accord with the emir of Gibellum by which he gave them horses and bezants and promised that he would no longer harass pilgrims on their way to the Holy Sepulchre.[20]

Duke Godfrey and the Count of Flanders rushed to the aid of Raymond of Saint-Gilles; then they encamped on the farther side of the river and took part in the siege of 'Arqah.[21] Meanwhile the above-mentioned heathens failed to appear. A few days later our troops rode toward Tripoli and sighted outside the city Arabs, Turks, and Saracens, whom they immediately pushed upon; and in the encounter our forces slaughtered the cream of Tripolitan nobility. The death toll and bloodletting was so great that water from the aqueduct seemed to flow blood red into the Tripolitan cisterns, thereby bringing grief and sorrow to the survivors, who were so frightened that they scarcely dared venture outside the city gate.[22]

At another time our soldiers rode past the valley of Sem and found cattle, asses, sheep, and countless other animals. Sixty crusaders separated from the others and found three thousand camels. They drove back all of the livestock to the Christian army and thus brought great joy to the Christian militia.[23] Our ships set anchor in a nearby port during the siege of 'Arqah bringing the best of trade in grain, wine, meat, oil, and barley,

[20] Tudebode has a fuller account of the agreement than the *Gesta*. The *Gesta* fails to mention the mission of the Bishop of Albara and the emir's promise of protection of pilgrims. Raymond d'Aguilers notes that the Bishop of Albara went to Gibellum. See Raymond d'Aguilers, p. 90; Bréhier, *Gesta*, p. 186.

[21] Godfrey and Robert of Flanders left Gibellum on March 12, 1099, and arrived at 'Arqah on March 14, 1099; *H Chr*. 360. Albert of Aachen charged that Raymond was paid by the emir of Gibellum to decoy Godfrey and Robert to 'Arqah. See Albert, p. 453; see our *Raymond IV*, p. 120, for a refutation.

[22] This attack took place on April 18, 1099; *H Chr*. 366. Raymond d'Aguilers has a full account of it. See Raymond d'Aguilers, pp. 104, 105.

[23] The foraging expedition took place at the end of April; *H Chr*. 369. The *Gesta* fails to mention sixty crusaders. See Bréhier, *Gesta*, p. 188.

so that a bountiful supply was available for all.[24] Pons of Balazun, Anselm of Ribemont, William Pichardus, and many others
unknown to me fell in happy martyrdom at this siege.[25] The
Christians besieged the afore-mentioned castle for three months
less one day. Here we celebrated Easter, four days before the
Ides of April.[26]

The king of Tripoli often sent emissaries to Raymond of
Saint-Gilles,[27] urging him to abandon the siege and make peace.
Count Raymond, Duke Godfrey, Count Robert of Flanders,
Robert the Norman, and other pilgrims were influenced by
these peace feelers, as well as by the sight of new produce coming from other areas, because we were eating fresh beans in the
middle of March and new grain in the middle of April. Consequently, the great and small held a council and agreed that it
was wise to resume the journey to Jerusalem with the new fruits.
So they all agreed to make peace with the king of Tripoli.

They took leave of 'Arqah and arrived before Tripoli on the
sixth day of the week on the thirteenth day of the incoming May,

[24] Raymond d'Aguilers states that ships from Antioch and Latakia, along
with Venetian and Greek vessels, anchored but sailed back to Latakia and
Tortosa. See Raymond d'Aguilers, p. 88. The words of the *Gesta* and Tudebode
are similar to Raymond but offer a shortened version.

[25] Pons of Balazun, probably a knight from the diocese of Viviers, wrote
jointly with Raymond d'Aguilers. There are several variants of his name:
Balon, Ballon, Baladun, to name a few. He was hit by a rock and killed at
'Arqah. Anselm of Ribemont was a lord of Ribemont, a region in the valley
of Oise near Saint-Quentin. We cannot identify William Pichard. Raymond
has a lengthy account of a vision of Anselm. See Raymond d'Aguilers, pp. 88-89.
Anselm was killed February 25, 1099; *H Chr.* 355.

[26] Easter was celebrated April 10, 1099; *H Chr.* 365. The chronology of
Tudebode is better than that of the *Gesta*, which has the crusaders celebrating
Easter before he reports the death of Anselm. The Tudebode account and the
Gesta version of events at 'Arqah are inadequate and in many ways are digests
of the history of Raymond d'Aguilers. The *Gesta* omits many details including
the trial of the Holy Lance. See Bréhier, *Gesta*, p. 190, fn. 3. None of the
champions of the *Gesta* have explained why a simple knight or a cleric or
both would have omitted such an important story. At least the *C* version of
Tudebode (British Museum Harley MS Latin 3904, two sides of a small folio)
has an interpolation of the ordeal and includes information which is not in
Raymond d'Aguilers. See Raymond d'Aguilers, pp. 93-103. The *B* version
of Tudebode (Bibliothèque Nationale, Paris, MS Latin 4892) gives notice of
the trial of the Holy Lance but omits the story.

[27] The *Gesta* omits the name of Raymond of Saint-Gilles and says that the
king of Tripoli sent messengers to the leaders. Bréhier, *Gesta*, p. 188. Raymond
d'Aguilers blames the Count of Saint-Gilles for delaying the journey to
Jerusalem. The *Gesta* and Tudebode do not take such a position. See our
Raymond IV, pp. 123-126.

where they remained for three days.[28] The king of Tripoli made
an agreement with Raymond of Saint-Gilles and the other lords
by which he immediately released more than three hundred
prisoners whom he had captured in prior battles. He also gave
to Count Raymond fifteen thousand bezants, fifteen high-priced
horses, and assured an abundant sale of horses, asses, bread, and
all necessary goods, thus insuring the entire Christian army of
plenty.[29] The king of Tripoli made an agreement with the
crusaders that if they were victorious in the forthcoming battle
which the emir was planning against them and could capture
Jerusalem, he would embrace Christianity and hold his lands
from the Christians. By such a meeting a convention was discussed and made.[30]

Afterwards the Christians departed from Tripoli on Monday
in the middle of May and crossed over a narrow and steep road
all day, and by night came to the castle of al-Batrūn.[31] Then they
approached a seacoast town called Gibelon,[32] where they suffered great thirst; and so worn-out the crusaders arrived at a
river named Brahim.[33] The crusading army then crossed, on the
day and night of the Ascension of the Lord,[34] a very narrow and
confined path where they anticipated an ambush, but by God's
grace not a foe appeared. Christ's army then went to the city of
Beirut, thence to Sidon, then on to Tyre,[35] and from Tyre

[28] The crusaders left 'Arqah on May 13 and remained before Tripoli for
three days; H Chr. 371.

[29] The Gesta again omits the name of Raymond of Saint-Gilles. Bréhier,
Gesta, p. 190. Raymond d'Aguilers wrote that earlier the king of Tripoli
had offered the leaders fifteen thousand gold pieces as well as horses, mules,
and goods. He wrote that after the Tripolitan defeat, the king of Tripoli
made a like promise and agreed to release Christian prisoners. See Raymond
d'Aguilers, pp. 91, 105.

[30] The emir of Babylon (Cairo) is not identified by Tudebode. He was
al-Afdal Shāhānshāh, the vizir of the Fatimid caliph. He had seized Jerusalem
on August 26, 1098, from the Turkish lords, Sokman and Il-Ghāzī ibn-Artuk.

[31] The town, al-Batrūn (Botrys, Botron) was south of Tripoli. The crusaders
left Tripoli on May 16, 1099, and arrived at al-Batrūn on the sixteenth or
seventeenth of May, 1099; H Chr. 372.

[32] Gibelon (Zebar in Gesta) was the ancient city of Byblos, now Jubail. Today
a crusader castle looks down on the ancient ruins. The mountains along the
coast are not high but are rugged enough to offer difficulties.

[33] This was the river Nahr-Ibrāhīm (Adonis). It flowed south of Byblos.

[34] The day of the Ascension was May 19, 1099; H. Chr. 373.

[35] The crusaders probably arrived at Beirut(Berytus, Bairūt) on May 19,
1099; H Chr. 373. The road between Beirut and Sidon(Sagitta, Saidā) offered
few difficulties. Later Saint Louis built his castle at Sidon. The crusaders

arrived at Acre; and from there they crossed near a castle called Caiphas and approached the city of Caesarea,[36] where they celebrated Pentecost May 29, 1099.[37] From there they arrived at Ramla,[38] which had been abandoned by the frightened Saracens at the approach of the Franks. In a nearby celebrated church lay the most precious body of Saint George,[39] who by the perfidy of the pagans underwent blessed martyrdom in the name of Christ.

All of our leaders at once assembled in order that they might faithfully elect a bishop who would guard and rehabilitate the church, and to whom they gave one-tenth of the gold, silver, animals, and horses so that the bishop could live most honorably with those who remained with him.[40] So he dwelled there in a state of bliss.

---

arrived there, May 20, 1099; *H Chr.* 374. They probably camped on the banks of the river, an-Nahr al-Auwalī. See Albert, p. 458. The crusaders arrived at Tyre(Sūr) on May 23, 1099; *H Chr.* 376. Crusaders from Antioch, Latakia, and Edessa joined the main army here. Raymond, the *Gesta,* and Tudebode do not have this information given by Ekkehard. See Ekkehard, p. 162, and our *Raymond IV,* p. 126. Raymond d'Aguilers indulges in a digression on the persecution of the Surians. See Raymond d'Aguilers, p. 109.

36 The crusaders arrived at Acre (Ptolemais, Saint John, 'Akkā) on May 24, 1099; *H Chr.* 377. Runciman thinks that Caiphas was Haifā (Caiphas, Caiffa) and that the crusaders passed by Mount Carmel. See Runciman, 1951: p. 276, and Hagenmeyer, *Gesta,* p. 444, fn. 19. The Christians arrived at Caesarea(Qaisārīyah) on May 26, 1099; *H Chr.* 378. The town was controlled by a Fatimid garrison. Raymond d'Aguilers relates that a pigeon fell into the Christian camp. See Raymond d'Aguilers, p. 114.

37 Pentecost was celebrated on May 29, 1099; *H Chr.* 379.

38 The crusaders entered Ramla(Rama, ar-Ramlah) on June 3, 1099; *H Chr.* 382.

39 Saint George was originally from Lydda, and his church was near Ramla.

40 The crusaders selected a Norman, Robert of Rouen, as bishop. The Christians remained at Ramla from June 3 to June 6, 1099; *H Chr.* 382, 383.

XI. The Capture of Jerusalem

RAYMOND OF SAINT-GILLES and Godfrey, along with other happy pilgrims, arrived before Jerusalem, rejoicing and boasting on Tuesday of the seventh day of entering June and set up a formidable siege.[1] Robert the Norman occupied the zone to the north next to the church of the Blessed Protomartyr, Stephen, where the saint happily for the name of Christ was stoned.[2] Adjoining his sector was that of the Count of Flanders; Duke Godfrey and Tancred[3] encamped to the west, while Raymond of Saint-Gilles took position on Mount Zion next to the church of the Blessed Mary, Mother of the Lord.[4] It was in this place that Mary departed the world, that the Lord broke bread with the disciples, and that the Holy Spirit entered the hearts of the disciples.[5]

On the third day of the siege knights of our army of the Holy Sepulchre, namely Raymond Pilet, Raymond of Turenne, and others moved out intent on plundering. The knights of Christ came upon two hundred Arabs, gave battle to the pagans, and with God's aid and that of the Holy Sepulchre overwhelmed

[1] The crusaders arrived at Jerusalem on June 7, 1099; *H Chr.* 385. Tudebode has the correct date. The *Gesta* has an incorrect date. The *Gesta* does not mention the arrival of Raymond of Saint-Gilles and Duke Godfrey. See Bréhier, *Gesta,* p. 194, fn. 1; Hagenmeyer, *Gesta,* p. 448, fn. 1. Jerusalem was ruled by Iftikhār-ad-Daulah.

[2] The Gate of Saint Stephen, located to the north, was named in honor of the protomartyr, Stephen, who was stoned to death. See *Actus Apostolorum* 6 & 7. The church was outside the walls of Jerusalem.

[3] Raymond d'Aguilers adds that Robert of Normandy was also encamped here. These leaders protected the area from Saint Stephen's church to an angular tower adjacent to the Tower of David, which was located to the west and guarded the Jaffa Gate. See Raymond d'Aguilers, p. 116.

[4] Mount Zion was located on the southwest corner of Jerusalem. Raymond d'Aguilers reports that the Count of Saint-Gilles moved his camp. Raymond d'Aguilers, p. 117.

[5] Tudebode has a few more details on Mount Zion than the *Gesta.* Raymond d'Aguilers gives even more information. The common source for the three chroniclers was the "Holy Places." The *Gesta* seems to delete from either Tudebode, Raymond, or the common source. See MS 5135 *A,* Folio 37b-39 (Bibliothèque Nationale, Paris), for a brief text, usually referred to as "Holy Places" and copied after the conclusion of texts of the *Gesta* and Tudebode, except in the case of the Berlin MS of the *Gesta,* which has lost the concluding folios, and therefore gives no evidence. Bréhier, *Gesta,* p. 194.

them, slaughtering many and seizing thirty horses.[6] On the second day of the following week (Monday) the crusaders launched such a staunch attack that Jerusalem would have fallen if scaling ladders had been available. However, they tumbled a lesser wall, pushed a ladder against a major wall, and our knights mounted it, and engaged the pagans in close combat with swords and lances.[7] Raginaldus, seneschal of Hugh of *Liziniacensis,* and many other Christians met death there, but the enemy casualties were heavier.[8]

For ten days the Christians were without bread,[9] when news came that our ships were anchored in a nearby port of Jaffa.[10] So at daylight one hundred knights from the army of Raymond of Saint-Gilles, including Raymond Pilet, Geldemar Carpinel, Achard of Montmerle, William of Sabran, and others whose names I do not know, left the siege.[11] When they marched to the

---

[6] This encounter took place on June 9, 1099; *H Chr.* 386. Tudebode writes of the army of the Holy Sepulchre and adds with the aid of the Holy Sepulchre.

[7] This attack was made on June 13, 1099; *H Chr.* 389. Raymond d'Aguilers has a similar account. See Raymond d'Aguilers, p. 117.

[8] We do not translate *Liziniacensis* as there are many place names in southern France formed on the proper name Licinius modified by suffixes. In this connection see A. Giry, 1894: pp. 385, 386, 409. Giry notes developments of place names in *-iacus, -iacum.* Grandgent, #39, notes adjective development from nouns using the suffix *-ensis.* Then these adjectives might be employed as nouns. Place names, particularly, employ the *-ensis* suffix and are declined as *ensis.* The *Gestà* does not mention Reginald, and the variant manuscripts of Tudebode mention that he was a seneschal of Hugh. See Hagenmeyer, *Gesta,* p. 454, fn. 12.

[9] Tudebode is very brief on food conditions. The *Gesta* has a fuller version of the thirst of the Christians, which is little more than a short summary of Raymond's long account. See Bréhier, *Gesta,* p. 196; Raymond d'Aguilers, pp. 118, 119.

[10] The Genoese fleet arrived at Jaffa (Joppa, Yāfā) on June 17, 1099; *H Chr.* 392. Raymond d'Aguilers reports the arrival of six ships. See Raymond d'Aguilers, p. 119. *Gesta* manuscripts and Tudebode manuscripts follow different spelling traditions for Jaffa. Bongars, *Gesta,* p. 27, writes *Iaphiae.* *Gesta* manuscripts write *-ie or -ię,* both indicating genitive feminine and a formation with the suffix *-ia.* See Schwan-Behrens #29,5; Grandgent, #37. Ioppe(dative), *-en*(acc.), *-e*(gen.) occur in the Vulgate. See *Actus Apostolorum* 9:36; 10:5; 11:5, indicating a usual adaptation from the Greek. Tudebode's *-i* genitive endings may suggest late Latin confusion of *-i, -e* in final syllables both in pronunciation and in spelling; Grandgent, #243, 244. The difference in textual tradition between Tudebode and the *Gesta* here suggests separate editorial histories.

[11] Geldemar Carpinel is not mentioned by the *Gesta.* Carpinel was on good terms with Godfrey and was given Haifa by Godfrey only to have Tancred prevent his possession. See Rey: 1869: p. 264. Achard of Montmerle (Canton

port thirty of our knights, among whom were Geldemar and
Achard, made a diversionary move and encountered six hundred
Arabs, Turks, and Saracens. The Christian knights charged
valiantly, but the superiority of the pagans over our men was
such that they hemmed the crusaders in on all sides, and killed
Achard of Montmerle and poor footmen.

While the Christians were so trapped that they only awaited
death, a messenger rushed to Raymond Pilet and questioned:
"Why do you dally here with your knights? Lo! All your comrades are in the clutches of Arabs, Turks, and Saracens, perhaps
even dead at this very minute. Hurry, hurry to their aid!" The
messenger's report brought the crusaders to life, and they rushed
hurriedly to the scene of the battle. The infidels formed two
lines when they sighted the Jerusalem knights. The Christians
countered by calling upon the name of Christ and the Holy
Sepulchre and hurled themselves so spiritedly against the foe
that every individual knight overcame his adversary. Realizing
that they were no match for the derring-do of the crusaders, the
enemy became paralyzed with fear, called retreat, and fled. Our
troops chased them almost four miles, killing numerous infidels,
and holding one alive as an informer. In addition they seized
one hundred and three horses.[12]

In the course of the siege scarcity of water plagued the crusaders so much that they stitched skins of oxen, buffalo, and
goats into leather bottles and lugged water in them for six miles.
Such foul and stinking water was drunk from these canteens that
daily we were in great misery and torment because of the fetid
water and barley bread. The Fountain of Siloam, situated at the
foot of Mount Zion, sustained us for the moment. But even the
water was sold among Christians of God and the Holy Sepulchre
so that one man could scarcely quench his thirst for a penny.
The Saracens, lying in ambush around all fountains and wells,
slew those whom they could find, and led away animals into

---

de Trévoux, Ain) mortgaged his property to Cluny to furnish himself for a
crusade. See Bréhier, *Gesta,* p. 14, fn. 5. William of Sabran was lord of
Sabran (Gard) and in the provençal army. See *HGL* 3: pp. 490-491; 5: cols.
687, 708, 732.

[12] Raymond d'Aguilers also describes this encounter. He reports two
hundred of the enemy were killed. The skirmish took place on June 18, 1099;
H Chr. 393; Raymond d'Aguilers, p. 120.

caverns, caves, or mountains. In other places the infidels slaughtered those who foraged in the vineyards.[13]

When our lords saw these atrocities, they were greatly angered and held a council in which the bishops and priests recommended that the crusaders hold a procession around the city. So the bishops and priests, barefooted, clad in sacred vestments, and bearing crosses in their hands, came from the church of the Blessed Mary, which is on Mount Zion, to the church of Saint Stephen, the Protomartyr, singing and praying that the Lord Jesus Christ deliver his holy city and the Holy Sepulchre from the pagan people and place it in Christian hands for His holy service.[14] The clerks, so clad, along with the armed knights and their retainers, marched side by side.

The sight of this caused the Saracens to parade likewise on the walls of Jerusalem, bearing insignia of Mohammed on a standard and pennon. The Christians came to the church of Saint Stephen and there took their stations as is customary in our processions. In the meantime the Saracens stood on the walls, screamed, blared out with horns, and performed all kinds of acts of mockery. To add insult to injury they made from wood a cross similar to the one on which, pouring forth His blood, the most merciful Christ redeemed the world. Afterward they inflicted great sorrow upon the Christians when, in the sight of all, they beat upon the cross with sticks and shattered it against the walls, shouting loudly, *"Frango agip salip,"* which means "Franks, is this a good cross?"[15]

---

[13] The three accounts, the *Gesta*, Raymond, and Tudebode report on the thirst of the Christians and the suffering at the Pool of Siloam. The wording of the three is close in places. Raymond writes that the crusaders carried water two or three leagues. The *Gesta* and Tudebode write six miles. Raymond reports that the water supply for one person cost five or six pennies(*nummi*). Tudebode reports one penny(*nummum*). See Raymond d'Aguilers, pp. 118, 119; *Liber*, pp. 139, fn. 4, 140: Bréhier, *Gesta* p. 198.

[14] His holy service (*Servicium faciendum*) was a feudal term. It was service or duty owed by the tenant to his lord. See Martin, 1892: p. 243.

[15] Tudebode has a more informative account of the procession than the *Gesta* and Raymond d'Aguilers. The *Gesta* dates the procession incorrectly. See Raymond d'Aguilers, pp. 122, 123; Bréhier, *Gesta,* p. 202, fn. 1. The council was held on July 6, 1099 (*H Chr.* 397) after Peter Desiderius gave celestial instructions. The procession was held on July 8, 1099; *H Chr.* 398. Tudebode's account is by far the best. He shows knowledge of the Holy Places and traces the route taken by the procession better than either the *Gesta* or Raymond d'Aguilers. Tudebode notes that the Saracens shouted *"Frango agip salip"* after they had shattered a cross. The editor of the *RHC,*

The Christians were greatly distressed by this sight, but continued with their prayers as they wound their way up in the procession to the church of the Mount of Olives, from which place Christ ascended to heaven. There a most respected clerk, Arnulf, preached a sermon elaborating on the mercy which God would bestow upon Christians who followed Him even to His grave, from which He mounted to heaven.[16] So the Saracens, seeing the Christians standing there in a most advantageous view, began to threaten them by running to and fro between the Temple of the Lord and the Temple of Solomon. But the Christians continued the procession and came to the monastery of the Blessed Mary in the Valley of Jehosaphat, from which her most holy body was snatched up to heaven. Thence they returned to the Mount of Olives in which place a clerk, wishing to enter the church when the procession came to the entrance of the monastery, was struck in the middle of his forehead and died on the spot. I believe his soul will dwell with Christ through eternity, world without end. Amen.[17] This is believed by him who first wrote this, since he was in the procession and saw it with his worldly eyes—namely, Peter Tudebode.[18]

Immediately thereafter our lords studied means by which they could take Jerusalem and enter the Sepulchre for the purpose of adoring their Lord and Saviour. They constructed two wooden towers and many other machines of war. Both Godfrey and Raymond of Saint-Gilles equipped their towers with war devices. Wooden beams for the construction of these towers had to be dragged from distant places. Fifty or sixty captive Saracens bore

---

Occ. 3: p. 105, in his Tudebode text, translates it in a footnote as *"Franci miranda(est) crux,"* although in his text he uses "franci est bona crux." The Tudebode manuscript *A* punctuates as a question and in its context a question makes sense, and we have translated, "Is this a good cross?" See Wehr, 1966: p. 521, *salib*(cross); p. 591, '*Ajib*(wonderful). William of Tyre follows the account of Tudebode rather closely. See William of Tyre, tr. Babcock and Krey, 1943: pp. 359, 360.

[16] This cleric was probably Arnulf of Chocques, chaplain of Robert of Normandy. He was also called Malecorne. He became patriarch in 1099. Raymond d'Aguilers disliked him and probably would not have mentioned his name any more than necessary. It is strange that a Norman knight would have neglected to include him in the *Gesta* account. Raymond's account overlooks the violence and attacks on the marchers. His version does not make sense as we noted in his book. See Raymond d'Aguilers, p. 123, fn. 13.

[17] This is a quotation drawn from *Apocalypsis B. Joannis* 11: 15, 16.

[18] This information testifies to Tudebode's presence. Variants of his name appear as *Tudebodis Subracensis* and *Sivracensis*.

the timbers on their shoulders, and thus the Christians disconcerted the enemy with their own men.[19] Sight of the building of these machines caused the Saracens to take extraordinary measures to fortify the city and to strengthen the towers by night and day.

On a certain day the enemy sent a Saracen for the purpose of spying on the building of war machines of the Christians. But Syrians and Greeks, seeing the Saracen, pointed him out to the crusaders, saying: *"Ma te Christo caco Sarrazin,"* which in our language means: "By Christ, this a dastardly Saracen." After grabbing him the Christians interrogated the Saracen through an interpreter asking him why he had come. In reply the captive said: "The Saracens sent me here to discover what were your inventions." In response the Christians pronounced judgment. They took the spy with bound hands and feet and placed him on the bottom of a machine called a petrary. They thought that with all of their might they could propel him within Jerusalem. They found it impossible, for he was ejected with such force that his bonds broke before he came to the walls and he was dismembered.[20]

After spotting the most vulnerable part of Jerusalem's defenses, the leaders, on a Saturday night, moved our war machines and wooden towers to the eastern sector of the siege.[21] At sunrise they erected them and for the next three days of the week put the towers in order and made them battle worthy. On the fourth and fifth days of the week they blitzed Jerusalem on all sides.[22] On the sixth day very early in the morning they again

[19] Tudebode notes the number of captive Saracens as does Raymond d'Aguilers. The *Gesta* is very brief at this point. Raymond has the most detailed account. See Raymond d'Aguilers, p. 124; Bréhier, *Gesta,* p. 200.

[20] *Ma te Christo caco Sarrazin* is described as broken Greek. See *RHC. Occ.* 3: p. 107. It is possible that the original source of this statement is oral and, consequently, interpretation on the basis of orthography is uncertain. Tudebode is the only writer to report the story of the captured spy.

[21] The crusaders moved and set up their towers and machines of war in a valley extending from the Gate of Saint Stephen to the valley of Jehosaphat. This action took place night of July 9, to July 12, 1099; *H Chr.* 399.

[22] The *Gesta* digresses at this point with the mention of thirst and the fact that one denarius was insufficient to quench a man's thirst. Tudebode has this information at the correct place, as does Raymond d'Aguilers. Tudebode uses one *nummum* rather than a denarius. The Latin of the three accounts is rather close. The general attack was made on July 13 and 14, 1099; *H Chr.* 403. See Bréhier, *Gesta,* p. 200.

assaulted the city, but became dumfounded and terrified when
their efforts availed them naught. Despite this setback, at the
approach of the hour in which our Lord Jesus Christ [23] decided
to be crucified on the Cross for us, our knights, Duke Godfrey,
and his brother Count Eustace, battled valiantly on a siege
tower. Then a knight named Lethold [24] scaled a wall of the
city, closely followed by our knights of Christ along with Count
Eustace and Duke Godfrey. The defenders scurried from the
wall and scattered throughout Jerusalem, while our men pursued them, killing, and lopping off heads.

In the meantime, Raymond of Saint-Gilles was stymied by a
deep ditch near the wall as he rolled his siege tower toward it.
After counseling on measures to be taken to fill the ditch, Raymond announced that anyone dumping three stones into the
ditch would be paid one denarius. Upon completion of the fill
after three days and two nights, the Christians moved the siege
tower next to one of the city towers.

The defenders struck back spiritedly against our forces with
fire and rocks so that they shattered the upper part of Raymond's
tower. So when the count and his knights were angered and
confused because the defenders had broken most of the upper
part of the tower and it appeared to be burning, he suddenly saw
three knights from the army of Duke Godfrey approaching from
the Mount of Olives and yelling that Duke Godfrey and his men
were in Jerusalem. At news of the Frankish break into Jerusalem, Raymond shouted to his men: "Why do you hang back?
Listen, all of the Franks are in the city." At this command they
picked up their ladders, pushed them against the wall, and thus
battling entered Jerusalem. [25]

The emir, who commanded the Tower of David, relinquished

[23] The crusaders entered Jerusalem on July 15, 1099; *H Chr.* 405. Raymond
d'Aguilers states that it was around midday. The *Gesta* and Tudebode use
the hour of the death of Christ, which was supposedly at three o'clock.
Bréhier, *Gesta*, p. 202, fn. 3, and Hagenmeyer, *Gesta*, p. 465, fn. 15, discuss
this at length. It is to be noted that the canonical service of nones might
be earlier than 3 P.M. and eventually became synonymous with noon or midday. It is interesting to note that Tudebode and the *Gesta* used a church hour
while Raymond uses midday. It is strange that a simple Norman knight
would have dated the event in such a manner.

[24] Lethold was supposedly from Tournai. Albert writes of his brothers,
Litholfus and Engilbertus. See Albert, p. 472.

[25] Tudebode has the best report of the activities of Raymond of Saint-Gilles.
The *Gesta* and Raymond d'Aguilers omit the account of three knights from
the army of Godfrey spreading the news of Godfrey's entry into Jerusalem.

it to Raymond of Saint-Gilles and opened the gate through which the pilgrims were accustomed to pay tribute. By this treaty Raymond agreed to conduct the emir and his retainers in the Tower of David safe and unharmed as far as Ascalon.[26] This he did. Upon entering Jerusalem the pilgrims pursued and killed Saracens and other infidels even to the Temple of Solomon and the Temple of the Lord. Gathered there the enemy waged a hot battle until sundown, but our men killed so many that blood flowed through all of the Temple.[27] Finally, after having overwhelmed the pagans, our men grabbed a large number of males and females in the Temple, killing some, and sparing others as the notion struck them. Tancred and Gaston of Béarn gave their banners to a great number of the infidels of both sexes crowded on the roof of the Temple.

Soon the crusaders ran through all the city taking gold, silver, horses, mules, and houses packed with all kinds of riches. Afterwards, all came rejoicing and weeping with joy to the Holy Sepulchre of our Saviour. On the next morning Tancred sent

---

The *Gesta* and Tudebode have an account of Raymond's payment for the filling of a ditch. Raymond d'Aguilers omits this bit of information, and is very sketchy on the count's role in the fall of Jerusalem. The *Gesta* relates that the count heard that the *Franci* were in the city, and then said: "Listen, all the *Francigene* are in the city." We have noted that *Franci* and *Francigene* are used interchangeably by the *Gesta*. In his account here Tudebode uses *Francigene* exclusively. We think that this is a good example of the uselessness of emphasizing the *Gesta's* use of *Francigene* at times as a mark of the Norman ancestry of the author. See Bréhier, *Gesta*, p. 204; Raymond d'Aguilers, p. 127; *-gena* was a popular suffix. *Alienigena* occurs in *Prophetia Ezechielis* 44:9. See also *verbigena, omnigena, terragena, Tropaire-Prosier* ed. Daux, 1901: pp. 74, 103, 108.

[26] The Tower of David was located to the west. Albert of Aachen accuses Raymond of Saint-Gilles of accepting a bribe from the emir, Iftikhār ad-Daulah. See Albert, pp. 483-489, and our *Raymond IV*, pp. 131, 132.

[27] Tudebode restricts himself to writing that blood flowed in the Temple in contrast with the *Gesta* and Raymond, who preferred to measure it. The *Gesta* writes in one place that the crusaders walked in blood to their ankles *(cavillas)*. He also wrote in another place that blood flowed in the Temple. The scribe of the *Gesta* seems to have followed Tudebode in one account and to have have followed Raymond d'Aguilers with reservations in another or the common source. Raymond d'Aguilers wrote that they rode in blood to the knees and bridles of their horses. *Apocalypsis B. Joannis* 14: 20 is the basis for these stories. See also *New Testament Apocrypha* 2, ed. Hennecke, 1964: p. 697. "And the blood from the swords shall reach even to the bellies of the horses." The account is also included in *Epistula Dagoberti Pisani archiepiscopi* in Hagenmeyer, 1901: p. 171, *usque ad genua equorum*. We cannot understand why writers of modern textbooks repeat this story without indicating its source, unless they are ignorant of it. Certainly there is strong evidence that the crusaders did not dispatch all of the natives. See Bréhier, *Gesta*, p. 202; Raymond d'Aguilers, pp. 127, 128.

forth the command that the Christians go to the Temple to kill Saracens.[28] Upon their arrival some began to draw their bows and to kill many. Another group of crusaders climbed to the roof of the Temple and rushed the Saracens huddled there, decapitating males and females with naked sword blades. They caused some to plunge from the Temple roof and others found their death above.

On another day [29] the Christians held a meeting before the Temple and agreed that each one should say prayers, give alms, and fast so that God would elect someone pleasing to Him to reign over the others, to govern Jerusalem, and to despoil the pagans. But the bishops and priests commanded that the crusaders first drag the bodies of Saracen dead from Jerusalem lest the unbearable stench harm them. Actually all of Jerusalem was clogged with cadavers. The Saracen survivors pulled out the corpses of their fellows to the gate exits, corded them up in mounds like houses, and put them to the torch.[30] Has anyone ever seen or heard of such a holocaust of infidels? God alone knows the number for no one else does.

Throughout the city Christians celebrated the Feast of the Octave of the capture of Jerusalem, and on the same day they held a council in which they elected Duke Godfrey prince of Jerusalem, so that he would battle the pagans and protect the Christians.[31] In a similar manner they selected a most wise and noted patriarch named Arnulf on the Feast of Saint Peter in Chains.[32] The city was captured on the fifteenth day of July, the sixth day of the week, with the aid of our Lord Jesus Christ to Whom is the honor and glory forever and forever. Amen.[33]

[28] The *Gesta* does not state that Tancred issued orders to kill Saracens within the Temple. The author states that he was angry when he received word of the massacre. See Bréhier, *Gesta*, p. 206; Hagenmeyer, *Gesta*, p. 474, fn. 43. If the *Gesta* was re-edited or was a copy of Tudebode, the better image of Tancred is understandable. Bréhier does not handle this problem.

[29] Tudebode writes "on another day." The *Gesta* is vague on time. The meeting was held on July 17, 1099; *H Chr.* 408.

[30] The *Gesta* neglects to state that the bodies were burned. See Bréhier, *Gesta*, p. 206. The *Gesta* has them corded up in mounds like houses but leaves them there. This example shows that the scribe failed to add, "put them to the torch," which was certainly necessary.

[31] Godfrey was elected on July 22, 1099; *H Chr.* 409. Raymond d'Aguilers states that the Count of Toulouse was offered the kingship, but that he refused to take it. See Raymond d'Aguilers, p. 129.

[32] Simeon, the patriarch of Jerusalem, died at Cyprus. Arnulf was elected on August 1, 1099; *H Chr.* 413.

[33] The *Gesta* omits the conclusion—"with the aid of our Lord Jesus Christ, to Whom is the honor and glory forever and forever. Amen."

XII. The Battle of Ascalon

IN THE MEANTIME a courier came to Tancred and Count
Eustace with instructions for them to make preparations to
move out to take Nablus. They did so, and accompanied by
many knights and footmen arrived at Nablus, where its inhabitants immediately turned over the city to them.[1] Then Duke
Godfrey through a messenger commanded Tancred and Godfrey's brother Eustace to rush to him because he had heard that
the emir of Babylon was in the city of Ascalon, where he was
making plans to capture Jerusalem.[2] He was even bringing
chains and other iron shackles with which he could fetter young
Christians, whom he would enslave for years. But he had
ordered all of the old Christians killed.

When Count Eustace and Tancred received this message, they
came with great joy through the mountains, eager for a fight
with the Saracens, and so arrived at Caesarea. Finally they
turned down the seacoast and came to Ramla, where they spotted
many Arabs who were in the vanguard of the approaching conflict. The Christians pursued and seized many captives who reluctantly related complete news on battle plans, location of the
enemy, size of their forces, and where they planned to fight.[3]
When Count Eustace and Tancred received this information,
they immediately dispatched to Jerusalem a courier with these
words to Duke Godfrey, the Patriarch Arnulf, and all of the
princes: "Know you, battle preparations are being made against
us in the city of Ascalon. For this reason hasten there with all
possible strength you can muster."

Duke Godfrey commanded all of the people to take energetic
steps to move to Ascalon against the enemies of God. Then
Godfrey, in company of the Patriarch, the Count of Flanders and

---

[1] Eustace of Boulogne was a brother of Godfrey. Nablus (Neapolis, Nābulus)
was north of Jerusalem. Tancred and Eustace had gone there during the
siege of Jerusalem. Their first expedition had been made July 10-13, and this
sortie was made on July 25, 1099; *H Chr.* 400, 410.

[2] Godfrey sent word on August 4, 1099; *H Chr.* 414. Ascalon(Ashkelon) was
located some forty miles southwest of Jerusalem. The emir of Babylon(Cairo)
was al-Afdal-Shāhānshāh.

[3] Tancred and Eustace arrived and the fight took place on August 7, 1099;
H Chr. 417.

the Bishop of Marturana, went out of Jerusalem on the third day of the week.[4] However, Raymond of Saint-Gilles and Robert the Norman said: "We shall not budge unless we are sure that there will be a battle."[5] Consequently, they commanded their men to move out and verify the report of an approaching encounter. If they found this true the counts ordered: "You return posthaste, and we shall be on the alert."

Their men reconnoitered, saw evidence of battle preparations, rushed back, and reported: "Certainly it is true because we have seen it with our own eyes." Afterwards Duke Godfrey sent the Bishop of Marturana to Jerusalem with commands to Raymond of Saint-Gilles, Robert the Norman, and other lords that they hurry to his side if they wished to engage the enemy. The Bishop of Marturana, returning with messages from the Patriarch and the duke, met Saracens who seized him and led him to a place unknown to us.[6]

Raymond and the other leaders left Jerusalem on the fourth day of the week; and prepared for battle, they marched to serve Godfrey.[7] Peter the Hermit remained in Jerusalem making arrangements and advising the Greeks and Latins for God's sake to form processions, offer prayers, and give alms so that God would bestow victory upon His people. So the clergy, barefooted, clad in sacred garments, and carrying crosses in their hands, made a procession from the Holy Sepulchre to the Tem-

[4] Godfrey and his associates left Jerusalem on August 9, 1099, *H Chr.* 418. The Bishop of Marturana was from Marturana in Calabria. He pushed the cause of Arnulf. See Raymond d'Aguilers, p. 131.

[5] The reluctance of Raymond of Saint-Gilles to leave at once does not reflect his quarrel with Godfrey. See our *Raymond IV*, p. 135, and Raymond d'Aguilers, pp. 132, 133.

[6] It is not clear just when the Bishop of Marturana was seized by the enemy. Raymond d'Aguilers reports his capture before he reports his mission from Godfrey. However, he infers that he was seized on his way to Jerusalem with dispatches from Godfrey. The Tudebode variants and the *Gesta* are clouded, but the inference is that the Bishop of Marturana was seized with messages *of* or *to* the duke. The Tudebode manuscripts place the march of Raymond on the fourth day of the week, after reporting the disappearance of the Bishop of Marturana as do the *Gesta* manuscripts with the exception of Madrid (which Bréhier considers most reliable) and MS Vatican 641. See Bréhier, *Gesta*, p. 210, fns. *g* and *h*.

[7] Tudebode writes Raymond of Saint-Gilles and others. The *Gesta* writes the princes. See Bréhier, *Gesta*, p. 210.

ple of the Lord with the litany and other prayers. So the clerics made a procession.[8]

Duke Godfrey, Raymond of Saint-Gilles, the Patriarch, other bishops, and all the remaining leaders gathered at a river which flows on this side of Ascalon.[9] There they found countless numbers of animals, oxen, camels, sheep, donkeys, and other cattle which the Saracens had sent out to hide. But the Christian knights and their retainers seized all of the animals.

At sundown the Patriarch, carrying with him the Cross of our Lord Jesus Christ, which the pilgrims had found in Jerusalem, and also the chaplain of Raymond of Saint-Gilles, carrying with him the Lance of our Lord Jesus Christ, began to order in the name of God, the Holy Sepulchre, the most precious Lance, and the most sacred Cross that no man should turn to any booty until the battle's end and the defeat of God's enemies. But afterwards they could return happily because of their good luck and great victory and seize whatever God had alloted to them.[10]

Because of these instructions the pilgrims of the Holy Sepulchre and the Christian knights at dawn on the sixth day of the week went into a beautiful valley nearby the seacoast and there arrayed their battle lines. Duke Godfrey, who had now been elected king of Jerusalem, drew up his lines; and likewise Raymond of Saint-Gilles, Robert the Norman, Robert of Flanders,

[8] The procession is reported more in detail by Raymond d'Aguilers. Tudebode and the *Gesta* mention Peter the Hermit as an organizer. Tudebode and Raymond note that the procession went to the Temple of the Lord. See Raymond d'Aguilers, pp. 132, 133.

[9] The armies met on August 11, 1099; *H Chr.* 420. The river was the Nahr-es- Safiyé between Jerusalem and Ascalon. See Bréhier, *Gesta,* p. 212, fn. 1.

[10] This episode is interesting. The *Gesta* does not state that the patriarch carried the Cross, or that the chaplain of Raymond of Saint-Gilles carried the Holy Lance. Tudebode and the *Gesta* are parallel in instructions of the patriarch against looting, but the *Gesta* does not state that Arnulf forbade such looting in the name of God, the Holy Sepulchre, the most precious Lance, and the most sacred Cross. Apparently the *Gesta* has a short version of these instructions. See Bréhier, *Gesta,* p. 212. Raymond d'Aguilers notes that the crusaders marched out of Jerusalem with the Holy Lance, but he fails to note that they carried the Cross. Earlier he had noted that Arnulf had led to the finding of the Cross. The Cross was supposedly found on August 5, 1099; *H Chr.* 415. Raymond also mentions briefly instructions concerning looting. He had noted similar instruction given by Peter Bartholomew on the eve of the battle with Kerbogha. See Raymond d'Aguilers, pp. 60, 133, 134. Tudebode has the best account and was certainly copying neither the *Gesta* nor Raymond.

Count Eustace, Tancred, and Gaston of Béarn formed their ranks. So six lines began to do battle while the archers were moving out front.[11] Joining them on the right and left flanks, all the animals, camels and other beasts moved out without a leader. The assistance of the animals was indeed a miracle of God.[12] Immediately the Christians began to fight in the name of Jesus Christ and of the Holy Sepulchre as they carried the Lance of our Saviour, and the Patriarch bore a part of the Cross of our Lord.

On the left flank was Duke Godfrey with his troops, and on the right side near the seacoast rode Raymond of Saint-Gilles. In the middle the Count of Normandy, the Count of Flanders, Count Eustace, Tancred, and Gaston of Béarn rode.[13] Then our troops began to move back and forth while the pagans stood at attention prepared for battle.

Each one of the enemy had a water bag strung to his neck to use while fighting the Christians. Count Robert of Flanders charged the enemy hotly, followed by Tancred and all of the others.[14] This sight caused the enemy to turn in flight at once. The battle was on a very large scale because the multitude of pagans was innumerable, and only God knew their number. But divine strength followed us and was so great and powerful that numbers counted little against our soldiers. The enemies of God stood blinded and stunned with open eyes staring at the

[11] The battle was fought on August 12, 1099; *H. Chr.* 421.

[12] The *Gesta* fails to mention the part played by the animals. However, Raymond d'Aguilers has a similar report. Sybel, who was not familiar with all of the Raymond manuscripts, thought that Raymond drew from the *Gesta* for his account of the battle of Ascalon. In view of the abbreviated account of Raymond and its similarity to Tudebode, it is more likely that Raymond's account of the battle of Ascalon was drawn from Tudebode or a common source rather than from the *Gesta*. The *B* manuscript of Raymond indicates that its account of Ascalon is drawn from another source. See *Liber*, p. 153 and fn. *r* Raymond d'Aguilers, p. 135.

[13] Raymond d'Aguilers states that they moved out in nine ranks. See Raymond d'Aguilers, p. 135.

[14] Tudebode does not mention the killing of the emir's standard-bearer by Robert of Normandy at the beginning of the battle as does the *Gesta*. He indicates later that Robert purchased the standard. Robert's act has been commemorated at Saint-Denis. See Bréhier, *Gesta*, pp. 214, 215, fn. 2. The discrepancy in the two accounts is ignored by Bréhier, and is another of many examples of differences in the two accounts.

Jerusalem knights of Christ, but seeing nothing and, trembling because of God's might, they dared not challenge the Christians.[15]

In their great fright they climbed and hid in trees, only to plunge from boughs like falling birds [16] when our men pierced them with arrows and killed them with lances. Later the Christians uselessly decapitated them with swords. Other infidels threw themselves to the ground groveling in terror at the Christians' feet. Then our men cut them to pieces as one slaughters cattle for the meat market. By the seacoast Raymond of Saint-Gilles put to the sword countless numbers, and those who could not flee plunged into the sea. Yet others fled to Ascalon.

The emir approached Ascalon in a dispirited and mournful state and bewailed his fate: [17] "Oh! Mohammed and our God,[18] who ever heard of such a catastrophe? Such might, such spirit, such fortitude,[19] such a hitherto invincible army in the face of Christian or pagan, now overwhelmed by such a puny people who could be squeezed to death in the fist [20] of anyone and overwhelmed. Alas! What sorrow and grief. What else can I say? [21] Why am I conquered by a mendicant people, unarmed and most miserably poor, who have neither scrip nor bag.[22] They now

---

[15] These lines are drawn from church lore. God blinded his enemies. See *Prophetia Ezechielis* 12:2, "Eyes to see and do not see"; *Liber Quartus Regum* 6:18; *Actus Apostolorum* 13:11, "The Lord made them blind and they could not see."

[16] Tudebode gives realism to his account by having the enemy to fall from trees as birds. The *Gesta* omits this information.

[17] The emir's lament, like the lament of Guy and the speech of Kerbogha's mother, is certainly a literary creation. Through all of them run ecclesiastical phrases. Bréhier does not deal with these creations except as interpolations apparently because he thinks that it belittles the historical value of the *Gesta*. He follows Sybel's dictum of leaving the false on one side and the true on the other. Unfortunately modern historical training deemphasizes the place of literature in history and thereby overlooks valuable clues. In this case Tudebode's account does not always parallel the *Gesta* version and is a fuller account. The more abbreviated *Gesta* could well have copied Tudebode and deleted part of his information, or again the two could have copied from a common source.

[18] The *Gesta* writes, "*O deorum spiritus,*" Tudebode writes, "*O Machomet et dii nostri.*" See Bréhier, *Gesta,* p. 216.

[19] *Tanta potestas, tanta virtus, tanta fortitudo* are church phrases. See Blaise, pp. 255, 284.

[20] *In pugillo;* see Hymn for Matins (*Quem terra pontus*), 15 August, Assumption of Blessed Virgin Mary (Common).

[21] "What else can I say?" is common. Raymond d'Aguilers likes to write *Quid plura?*

[22] It was common to question fate. This lament reminds us of Job.

chase our Egyptian people, who often gave them charity when they begged throughout our fatherland in ancient times. To this place I led a great force of knights and footmen including Turks, Saracens, Arabs, Agulani, Kurds, Asurpates, Azymites, and other pagans, whom I now see basely scurrying away on unbridled steeds on the road back to Cairo and who dare not return to face this frail race.[23] So I swear by Mohammed and the names of all of our gods that I shall no longer retain knights by compact because I have been overthrown by this most indolent people. I brought all kinds of arms and apparatus such as machines, and many iron chains [24] with which I thought I could lead the Christians back to Cairo in manacles. All of these preparations I made that I might besiege them in Jerusalem. Instead they came against me two days' journey from Jerusalem. What would have happened to me if I had led my men to the Holy City? [25] Certainly I believe that neither I nor any of my men could have fled from the place. What more can be said? I shall always be disgraced in the land of Cairo."

One of our men seized the standard of the emir. Above the standard was a golden apple on a spear, all encased in silver. Incidentally a standard is called a banner by us. Count Robert of Normandy bought the standard for twenty marks of silver and, in turn, gave it to the Patriarch in honor of God and the Holy Sepulchre.[26] A pilgrim also bought the sword of the emir

---

[23] The *Gesta* writes that the emir led two hundred thousand men. The author does not mention Turks, Saracens, Arabs, Agulani, Kurds, Asurpates, Azymites, and other pagans. Tudebode includes the above names. These have been discussed with the exception of the Asurpates, *La Chanson d'Antioche* 2: p. 246, mentions a people named Acopart which is, perhaps, the Asurpates of Tudebode. The *Gesta* writes that the men of the emir did not dare to return to face the *gentem Francigenam*. Tudebode writes *fragilem gentem* (frail race), which makes more sense at this point. See Bréhier, *Gesta*, p. 216.

[24] The *Gesta* makes no mention of the emir carrying manacles.

[25] Tudebode and Bongars *Gesta* p. 29, write: "What would have happened to me?" However, the Bongars text fails to mention Jerusalem and so is incomplete. The Tudebode text reads: "What would have happened to me if I had led my men to the Holy City?" Again we have evidence of Bongars' use of Tudebode. The other *Gesta* manuscripts do not include this. See Bréhier, *Gesta*, p. 216, fn. g.

[26] Tudebode does not give credit to Robert for the killing of the emir's standard-bearer. See above chap. XII, n. 14. If Tudebode had copied the *Gesta*, it is strange that he would have omitted this information. Actually, the *Gesta's* report of Robert's feat is out of place in the battle sequence. Bréhier has a rather unconvincing explanation in which he explains that a soldier seized the standard after Robert had killed the standard-bearer. It

for sixty bezants. Thus by God's approval all of our enemies were uniformly overwhelmed because they had no more fight left in them. The fleet from all the lands of the infidels lay in harbor there, when the sight of the rout of the emir and his army caused them to hoist sails at once, to take the emir aboard, and put out to the high seas.

Our soldiers returned to the enemy tents and seized huge amounts of gold, silver, garments, and a pile of many goods, in addition to horses, mules, camels, sheep, cattle, asses, and many other animals. Actually all the mountains, hills, and plains were covered with great numbers of their animals. The Christians also found a great cache of arms and proceeded to carry away those things they desired and to pile together those which they did not want and put them to the torch. Then our soldiers returned joyously and gladly, having conquered all of the pagans, and brought back many spoils with them such as camels, asses loaded with biscuits, flour, grain, cheese, bread, oil, and all essential goods.[27]

Because of this booty there was such an abundance among the Christians that an ox could be bought for eight or ten *nummi,* a peck of grain for twelve *nummi,* and a peck of barley for eight *nummi.*[28] For fear that this is not known to all Christians,[29] let them be informed that this battle was fought the day before the Ides of August by the grace of our Lord Jesus Christ, to Whom is the honor and glory now and forever throughout eternity. Amen.

---

seems rather improbable that Robert would have failed to claim the standard as his own. See Bréhier, *Gesta,* p. 217, fn. 5.

[27] The crusaders returned on August 13, 1099; *H. Chr.* 422.

[28] The *Gesta* quotes none of these prices. Tudebode seems to be unable to end his story and apparently has information not available to the *Gesta* or Raymond.

[29] The *Gesta* is abrupt and dates the battle without a transition. Tudebode writes, "For fear that this not known to all Chrisians, let them be informed," and then gives the date of the battle of Ascalon. See Bréhier, *Gesta,* p. 218.

IMPORTANT DATES

November 27, 1095. Urban preaches the First Crusade in Clermont.

August 1, 1096. Arrival of Peter the Hermit at Constantinople.

August 10, 1096. Peter the Hermit arrives at Nicomedia.

August 11, 1096. Peter the Hermit arrives at Civetot.

September 24, 1096. The crusaders occupy Xerigordon.

September 29, 1096. The Turks ambush a crusading force.

September 29- October 7, 1096. Siege of the fortification, Xerigordon, by the Turks.

Early part of October, 1096. Peter the Hermit returns to Constantinople.

October 21, 1096. The Turks attack Civetot.

November 1, 1096. Bohemond arrives at Avlona.

December 20, 1096- January 31, 1097. Provençals march across Sclavonia.

December 23, 1096. Arrival of Duke Godfrey at Constantinople.

Christmas, 1096. Bohemond celebrates Christmas at Kastoria.

Middle of February, 1097. Attack on Adhémar.

April 1, 1097. Normans arrive at Roussa.

April 10, 1097. Meeting of Alexius and Bohemond.

April 12, 1097. The Provençals capture Roussa.

April 21, 1097. Raymond of Saint-Gilles arrives at Constantinople.

April 26, 1097. The Norman army arrives at Constantinople.

May 14, 1097. Opening of the siege of Nicaea.

May 16, 1097. The Provençal army besieges Nicaea.

June 10, 1097. The sapping of a tower of Nicaea.

June 19, 1097. The surrender of Nicaea.

June 26-28, 1097. Departure of the crusaders from Nicaea.

July 1, 1097. The battle of Dorylaeum.

September 14, 1097. Tancred and Baldwin leave the main army and journey to Tarsus.

October 20-22, 1097. Opening of the siege of Antioch.

February 9, 1098. Defeat of the forces of Ridvan.

Early part of February, 1098. Taticius abandons the siege.

March 20, 1098. Completion of *La Mahomerie*.

May 29, 1098. Crusading princes make an agreement with Bohemond.

June 3, 1098. The Christians capture Antioch.

June 5, 1098. The main army of Kerbogha approaches Antioch.

June 28, 1098. Defeat of Kerbogha.

August 1, 1098. Death of Adhémar.

November 5, 1098. Council of crusaders held the church of Saint Peter in Antioch.

December 11-12, 1098. Capture of Ma 'arrat-an-Nu'mān.

January 4, 1099. Council of princes argue date of resumption of the march to Jerusalem.

January 13, 1099. Raymond of Saint-Gilles resumes the journey to Jerusalem.

February 14- May 13, 1099. Siege of 'Arqah.

April 8, 1099. Ordeal of the Holy Lance.

May 16, 1099-June 6. The crusaders journey to Jerusalem.

June 7, 1099. The Christians approach Jerusalem.

July 8, 1099. Christian procession around Jerusalem.

July 13-15, 1099. Final assault and capture of Jerusalem.

July 22, 1099. Election of Godfrey.

August 12, 1099. Battle of Ascalon.

ABBREVIATIONS

Albert— Albertus Aquensis, *Historia Hierosolymitana* in *Recueil des historiens des croisades: historiens occidentaux* 4 (Paris, 1879).

Bartsch— Bartsch, Karl. 1920. *Chrestomathie de l'ancien français* (Leipzig).

Blaise— Blaise, Albert. 1966. *Le Vocabulaire Latin des principaux thèmes liturgiques* (Turnhout).

Bongars, *Gesta*— *Gesta Dei per Francos sive orientalium expeditionem et regni Francorum Hierosolymitani historia a variis sed illius aevi scriptoribus litteris commendata*, edited by Jacques Bongars (Hanau, 1611).

Bréhier, *Gesta*— *Histoire anonyme de la première croisade*, edited by Louis Bréhier (1924).

La Chanson d'Antioche— edited by Paulin Paris (2 v., Paris, 1848).

Ekkehard— Ekkehardus Uraugiensis abbas, *Hierosolymita*, edited by Heinrich Hagenmeyer (Tübingen, 1877).

Grandgent— Grandgent, C. H. 1962. *An Introduction to Vulgar Latin* (New York).

Hagenmeyer, *Gesta*—*Anonymi gesta Francorum et aliorum Hierosolymitanorum* edited by Heinrich Hagenmeyer (Heidelberg, 1890).

H Chr.— Hagenmeyer, Heinrich, 1902-1911. *Chronologie de la première croisade, 1094-1100. Revue de l'Orient latin*, 6-8.

HGL— Devic, Dom. Cl. and Dom. J. Vaissete. 1872-1893. *Histoire générale de Languedoc* (15 v., Toulouse).

Liber— Raimundus de Aguilers, *Le Liber de Raymond d'Aguilers*, edited by John Hugh and Laurita L. Hill in *Documents relatifs à l'histoire des croisades publiés* par L'Académie des inscriptions et belles-lettres (Paris, 1969).

MPL— *Patrologiae cursus completus: Series Latina*, edited by J. P. Migne (Paris, 1844-1864).

Raymond d'Aguilers— Raimundus de Aguilers, *Historia Francorum qui ceperunt Iherusalem*, edited and translated by John Hugh and Laurita L. Hill, *Mem. Amer. Philos.* 71 (Philadelphia, 1968).

Raymond IV— John Hugh and Laurita L. Hill. 1962. *Raymond IV, Count of Toulouse* (Syracuse).

RHC Occ.— *Recueil des historiens des croisades:historiens occidentaux* 4 (Paris, 1844-1895).

Schwan-Behrens— Schwan-Behrens. 1932. *Grammaire de l'ancien Français* translated by Oscar Bloch (Leipzig).

Troper— *The Winchester Troper from MSS of the Xth and XIth Centuries*, edited by Walter Howard Frere in *Henry Bradshaw Society* 8 (London, 1894).

BIBLIOGRAPHY

SOURCES

Acta sanctorum quotque toto orbe coluntur, vel a Catholicis scriptoribus celebrantur (Antwerp, Paris, Rome, Brussels, 1643-1940).

The Alexiad of the Princess Anna Comnena, translated by Elizabeth A. S. Dawes (London, 1928).

ALBERTUS AQUENSIS. *Historia Hierosolymitana* in *Recueil des historiens des croisades: historiens occidentaux* 4 (Paris, 1879).

Ambroise, *L'Estoire de la Guerre Sainte* edited and translated by Gaston Paris (Paris, 1897).

AMBROSE. *De Excidio Urbis Hierosolimitanae* in *Patrologiae cursus completus: Series Latina*, 15 edited by J. P. Migne (Paris, 1844-1864).

———— *De Excessu fratris sui Satyri* in *MPL* 15.

———— *Epistolae* in *MPL* 16.

Anonymi gesta Francorum et aliorum Hierosolymitanorum, edited by Heinrich Hagenmeyer (Heidelberg, 1890).

Anonymi Gesta Francorum, edited by B. A. Lees (Oxford, 1924).

Baldricus Dolensis. *Historia Jerosolimitana* in *RHC Occ.* 4 (Paris, 1879).

Biblia Sacra (Rome, 1947).

Breviarium Romanum (4 v., Ratisbonae, 1923).

La Chanson de la croisade Albigeoise, edited and translated by E. Martin-Chabot. In: *Les Classiques de l'histoire de France au Moyen Age* 1 (Paris, 1931).

La Chanson d'Antioche, edited by Paulin Paris (2 v., Paris, 1848).

La Chanson d'Antioche Provençale ed. & trs. Paul Meyer in *Archives de l'Orient Latin* 2 (Paris, 1884).

La Chanson de Roland, edited and translated by Léon Gautier (Tours, 1887).

COMNENA, ANNA. *Alexiade. Règne de l'empereur Alexis I* Comnène (1081-1181), edited by B. Leib in *Collection byzantine de l'Association Guillaume* Budé (Paris, 1937-1945).

La Conquête de Jerusalem, edited by C. Hippeau (Paris, 1868).

RHC: Documents Armeniéns 1 (Paris, 1869).

EGINHARD. *Vie de Charlemagne*, edited and translated by Louis Halphen, in *Les classiques de l'histoire de France au Moyen Age* (Paris, 1923).

EKKEHARDUS URAUGIENSIS ABBAS. *Hierosolymita*, edited by Heinrich Hagenmeyer (Tübingen, 1877).

English Kalendars before A.D. 1100, edited by Francis Wormwald. In: *Henry Bradshaw Society* 72 (London, 1934).

FULCHER OF CHARTRES. *A History of the Expedition to Jerusalem, 1095-1127*, edited by Harold S. Fink and translated by Frances Rita Ryan (Knoxville, 1969).

FULCHERIUS CARNOTENSIS. *Historia Hierosolymitana. Gesta Francorum Iherusalem Peregrinantium* in *RHC Occ.* 3 (Paris, 1866).

———— *Historia Hierosolymitana. Gesta Francorum Iherusalem Peregrinantium*, edited by Heinrich Hagenmeyer (Heidelberg, 1913).

Gesta Dei per Francos sive orientalium expeditionum et regni Francorum Hierosolymitani historia a variis sed illius aevi scriptoribus litteris commendata, edited by Jacques Bongars (Hanau, 1611).

Gesta Francorum et aliorum Hierosolymitanorum. The Deeds of the Franks and other Pilgrims to Jerusalem, edited and translated by Rosalind Hill (London, 1962).

GUIBERTUS NOVIGENTUS. *Historia quae dicitur Gesta Dei per Francos* in *RHC Occ* 4 (Paris, 1789).

HAGENMEYER, HEINRICH. *Die Kreuzzugsbriefe aus den Jahren 1088-1100* (Innsbruck, 1901).

Histoire anonyme de la première croisade, edited and translated by Louis Bréhier in *Les Classiques de l'histoire de France au Moyen Age* 4 (Paris, 1924).

Missale Romanum Mediolani 1474, edited by Robert Lippe in *Henry Bradshaw Society* 17, 33 (London, 1899, 1907).

New Testament Apocrypha, edited and translated by Edgar Hennecke (2 v., Philadelphia, 1964).

Notitiae duae Lemovicensis de praedicatione crucis in Aquitania. In *RHC Occ* 5 (Paris, 1895).

RABANUS MAURUS. *De Universo.* In: *MPL* 111.

RADULPHUS CADOMENSIS. *Gesta Tancredi in expeditione Hierosolymitana.* In: *RHC Occ* 3 (Paris, 1866).

RAIMUNDUS DE AGUILERS. *Historia Francorum qui ceperunt Iherusalem,* edited and translated by John Hugh and Laurita L. Hill. *Mem. Amer. Philos.* 71 (Philadelphia, 1968).

——— *Le "Liber" de Raymond d'Aguilers,* edited by John Hugh and Laurita L. Hill. In: *Documents relatifs à l'histoire des croisades* publiés par *L'Académie des inscriptions et belles-lettres* (Paris, 1969).

——— *Historia Francorum qui ceperunt Iherusalem.* In: *RHC Occ* 3 (Paris, 1866).

ROBERTUS MONACHUS. *Historia Hierosolymitana.* In: *RHC Occ* 3 (Paris, 1866).

Sarum Missal, edited by J. W. Legg (Oxford, 1916).

The Testament of Abraham, edited by W. E. Barnes (Cambridge, 1892).

Tropaire-Prosier de l'abbaye Saint-Martin de Montauriol, edited by abbé Camille Daux in *Bibliothèque Liturgique* 9 (Paris, 1901).

The Winchester Troper from MSS of the Xth and XIth Centuries, edited by Walter Howard Frere. In: *Henry Bradshaw Society* 8 (London, 1894).

TUDEBODUS, PETRUS. *Historia de Hierosolymitana itinere,* edited by John Besly. In: *Historia Francorum scriptores,* edited by *A.* Duchesne 4 (Paris, 1641).

——— *Historia de Hierosolymitano itinere.* In: *RHC Occ* 3 (Paris, 1866).

WILLELMUS TYRENIS ARCHIEPISCOPUS. *Historia rerum in partibus transmarinis gestarum.* In: *RHC Occ* 1 (Paris, 1844).

WILLIAM OF TYRE. *A History of Deeds Done Beyond the Seas,* translated by E. A. Babcock and A. C. Krey (New York, 1943).

Notes referring simply to Missal, Office, or Breviary are cited according to standard divisions of these works found in the *Breviarium Romanum* and *Missale Romanum,* Latin, English, or combined versions.

PRINTED WORKS

ADAMS, EDWARD L. 1913. *Word Formation in Provençal* (New York).

ANDRESSOHN, J. C. 1947. *The Ancestry and Life of Godfrey of Bouillon* (Bloomington).

APPEL, CARL. 1902. *Provenzalische Chrestomathie* (Leipzig).

ARBELLOT, ABBÉ. 1881. *Les Chevaliers Limousins à la première croisade* (Paris).

BARTSCH, KARL. 1920. *Chrestomathie de l'ancien français* (Leipzig).

BÉDIER, JOSEPH. 1908-1913. *Les légendes épiques, recherches sur la formation des chansons de geste* (4 v., Paris).

BLAISE, ALBERT. 1966. *Le Vocabulaire Latin des principaux thèmes liturgiques* (Turnhout).

BRITT, MATTHEW. 1936. *The Hymns of the Breviary and Missal* (New York).

BRUNDAGE, JAMES T. 1959. "Adhémar of Puy. The Bishop and His Critics." *Speculum* 34.

───── 1960. "An Errant Crusader: Stephen of Blois." *Traditio* 16.

───── 1964. "Recent Crusade Historiography: Some Observations and Suggestions." *Catholic Hist. Rev.* 49.

CRÉGUT, G. REGIS 1895. *Le concile de Clermont en 1095 et la première croisade* (Clermont-Ferrand).

DAVID, CHARLES W. 1920. *Robert Curthose, Duke of Normandy* (Cambridge).

DESCHAMPS, PAUL. 1934. *Les Châteaux des croisés en Terre Sainte: le Crac des Chevaliers* (Paris).

DEVIC, DOM. CL. and DOM. J. VAISSETE. 1872-1893. *Histoire générale de Languedoc* (15 v., Toulouse).

DOWNEY, GLANVILLE. 1961. *A History of Antioch in Syria* (Princeton).

DUKE, MAY GRAHAM MATTHEWS. 1967. "A Study of the Problems of Authorship and Style of the *Gesta Francorum et aliorum Hierosolymitanorum*" (unpublished thesis, University of Houston).

DUNCALF, FREDERIC. 1921. "The Peasants' Crusade." *Amer. Hist. Rev.* 26.

DUSSAUD, RENÉ. 1927. *Topographie historique de la Syrie antique et médiévale* (Paris).

EBERSOLT, JEAN. 1921. *Sanctuaires de Byzance* (Paris).

GAVIGAN, JOHN JOSEPH. 1943. *The Syntax of the Gesta Francorum.* In: *Supplement to Language* (Baltimore).

GIRY, A. 1894. *Manuel de diplomatique* (Paris).

GRANDGENT, C. H. 1962. An *Introduction to Vulgar Latin* (New York).

GROUSSET, RENÉ. 1934-1936. *Histoire des croisades et du royaume franc de Jérusalem* (3 v., Paris).

HAGENMEYER, HEINRICH. 1902-1911. "Chronologie de la première croisade, 1094-1100. *Revue de l'Orient latin* 6-8.

───── 1879. *Peter der Eremite. Ein kritischer Beitrag zur Geschichte des ersten Kreuzzuges* (Leipzig).

HILL, JOHN HUGH. 1951. "Raymond of Saint-Gilles in Urban's Plan of Greek and Latin Friendship." *Speculum* 26.

HILL, JOHN HUGH and LAURITA L. 1955. "Contemporary Accounts and the Later Reputation of Adhémar, Bishop of Puy." *Medievalia et Humanistica* 9.

HILL, JOHN HUGH and LAURITA L. 1953. "The Convention of Alexius Comnenus and Raymond of Saint-Gilles." *Amer. Hist. Rev.* 58.

HILL, JOHN HUGH and LAURITA L. 1954. "Justification historique du titre de Raymond de Saint-Gilles: 'Christiane milicie excellentissimus princeps.'" *Annales du Midi* 66.

HILL, JOHN HUGH and LAURITA L. 1959. *Raymond IV de Saint-Gilles 1041 (ou 1042) -1105. Bibliothèque Méridionale, Série historique* 35 (Toulouse).

HILL, JOHN HUGH and LAURITA L. 1962. *Raymond IV, Count of Toulouse* (Syracuse).

HILL, JOHN HUGH and LAURITA L. 1960. *L'Allégorie chrétienne dans les récits relatifs au Wineland."* *Le Moyen Age* n. 1-2.

IORGA, NICOLAS. 1928. *Les Narrateurs de la première croisade* (Paris).

JAURGAIN, JEAN DE. 1902. *La Vasconie, étude historique et critique sur les origines du royaume de Navarre, du duché de Gascogne, des comtés de Comminges, d'Aragon, de Foix, de Bigorre, d'Alava et de Biscaye, de la vicomté de Béarn et des grand fiefs du duché de Gascogne* 2 (Pau).

KNAPPEN, MARSHALL M. 1928. "Robert II of Flanders in the First Crusade." *The Crusades and other Historical Essays Presented to Dana C. Munro* (New York).

KREY, A. C. 1958. *The First Crusade* (Gloucester).

―――― 1928. "A Neglected Passage in the Gesta and its Bearing on the Literature of the First Crusade." *The Crusades and other Historical Essays Presented to Dana C. Munro* (New York).

―――― 1948. "Urban's Crusade, Success or Failure?" *Amer. Hist. Rev.* 53.

LANGLOIS, ERNEST. 1904. *Table des noms propre de toute nature compris dans les chansons de geste* (Paris).

LEWIS, ARCHIBALD L. 1972. "The Economic and Social Development of the Balkan Peninsula during *Comneni* Times A.D. 1081-1185." *Actes du IIe Congrès International des Etudes du Sud-Est Européen* 2.

MARTIN, TRICE. 1892. *The Record Interpreter* (London).

MAYER, HANS EBERHARD. 1960. *Bibliographie zur Geschichte der Kreuzzüge* (Hannover).

―――― 1965. *Geschichte der Kreuzzüge* (Stuttgart).

―――― 1960. "Zur Beurteilung Adhemars von Le Puy." *Deutsches Archiv*, n. 2.

MUNRO, DANA C. 1906. "The Speech of Pope Urban II at Clermont, 1095." *Am. Hist. Rev.* 11.

NESBITT, JOHN W. 1963. "The Rate of March of Crusading Armies in Europe." *Traditio* 19.

NICHOLSON, ROBERT LAWRENCE. 1940. *Tancred: A Study of His Career and Work in Their Relation to the First Crusade and the Establishment of the Latin States in Syria and Palestine* (Chicago).

PARIS, GASTON. 1880. "La Chanson du pélerinage de Charlemagne." *Romania* 9.

REY, EDOUARD G. 1869. *Les Familles d'outre-mer de du Cange* (Paris).

RUINART, THIERRI. 1881. *Vita Urbani, MPL 151.*

RUNCIMAN, STEVEN. 1951. *A History of the Crusades* 1 (Cambridge).

SAULCY, F. DE. 1842. "Tancrède." *Bibliothèque de l'Ecole des Chartes* 4.

SCHWAN-BEHRENS. 1932. *Grammaire de l'ancien Français*, translated by Oscar Bloch (Leipzig).

SYBEL, HEINRICH VON. 1841. *Geschichte des ersten Kreuzzuges* (Dusseldorf).

―――― 1861. *The History and Literature of the First Crusade*, translated by Lady Duff Gordon (London).

THROOP, PALMER A. 1940. *Criticism of the Crusades, A Study of Public Opinion and Propaganda* (Amsterdam).

THUROT, CH. 1876. "Historiens de la première croisade." *Revue Historique* 1.

WEHR, HANS. 1966. *A Dictionary of Modern Written Arabic* (Ithaca).

YEWDALE, RALPH BAILEY. 1917. *Bohemond I, Prince of Antioch* (Princeton).

We acknowledge the unpublished theses of our students although the topics are not pertinent to this study—Dianne Lewis, "Incredible Elements in the Contemporary Chronicles of the Crusades," 1971; James Daniels, "A Study of the Method and Style of Ralph of Caen," 1972. We look forward to completion of further studies on William of Tyre and *La Chanson d'Antioche* by our students Jerry Skains and Maria Fernandez. Like mediaeval chroniclers we happily end the book with thanks to Tudebode for giving us a subject and to Renaud for whom we grieved in Istanbul and Anatolia and who gave cheer while we toiled amid the snows of Princeton.

INDEX

Adhémar, bishop of Le Puy, enters Sclavonia, 27; attacked by a band of Pechenegs, 28; arrives at the siege of Nicaea, 31; troops sap a tower, 33; attacks Turks at Dorylaeum, 36; loses his seneschal, 46; carries the Holy Lance into battle against Kergogha, 86; dies at Antioch, 93

al-Afdal Shāhānshāh, vizir of Egypt, leads an army against the Christians, 121; gives a lament over his defeat, 125; flees from the crusaders, 127

Alexius Comnenus, Byzantine emperor, quarrels with Godfrey, 23; receives Bohemond, 27; receives Raymond of Saint-Gilles, 29; promises Bohemond lands, 30; orders alms for the poor, 33; abandons the crusaders to their fate, 83

Amatus, archbishop of Bordeaux, accompanies Urban, 15

Andrew, Saint, reveals hiding place of the Holy Lance, 76

Anselm of Ribemont, loses his life at 'Arqah, 109

Antioch, crusaders besiege, 43; falls, 65; description of the city, 96; kings of the city, 97

Arnold Tudebode, loses his life, 93

Arnulf of Chocques, chaplain of Robert of Normandy, selected patriarch, 120; marches with Godfrey to Ascalon, 121; carries a part of the Cross, 124

'Arqah, besieged by the Christians, 106

Arvedus Tudebode, dies from wounds, 72-73

Ascalon, reports of the arrival of al-Afdal Shāhānshāh there, 121

Baldwin, brother of Godfrey, enters Hungary, 17; enters the valley of Botrenthrot, 39; quarrels with Tancred at Tarsus, 40

Beirut, arrival of the crusaders there, 110

Bohemond, Norman crusader, son of Robert Guiscard, besieges Amalfi, 23; takes the Cross, 24; arrives at Andronopolis, 25; celebrates Christmas at Castoria, 25; arrives at Roussa, 26;

confers with Alexius, 27; participates in the siege of Nicaea, 31; fights at Dorylaeum, 34-36; raids Saracen lands, 45; marches to Saint-Simeon and is attacked on his return to Antioch, 53; proposes to deliver Antioch, 61; connives with Fīrūz, 62; enters Antioch, 64; puts the quarters of Yaghi Siyan to the torch, 78; helps to defeat Kerbogha, 86; returns to Antioch after an illness, 95; feuds with Raymond of Saint-Gilles, 95; participates in the siege of Ma'arrat-an-Nu'mān, 98; quarrels with Raymond of Saint-Gilles at Chastel-Rouge, 102; expels Provençals from strongholds in Antioch, 102; arrives at Latakia, 107; returns to Antioch, 107

Camela, messengers from the city bring news to Raymond of Saint-Gilles, 106

Dorylaeum, site of battle, 34

Durazzo (Dyrrachium), Byzantine port, 22

Eustace, brother of Godfrey, pronounces judgment, 95; attacks Jerusalem, 118; occupies Nablus, 121; fights at Ascalon, 124

Fīrūz, agrees to deliver Antioch, 61

Fountain of Siloam, furnishes water for the crusaders, 114

Gaston of Béarn guards La Mahomerie, 57; gives banner to infidels at the Temple of Solomon, 119; fights at Ascalon, 124

Geldemar Carpinel, engages Arabs in conflict, 114

Geoffrey, count of Russignolo, engages Greek mercenaries in battle, 25

Gibelon, seacoast town, crusaders arrive there, 110

Godfrey, duke of Lorraine, enters Hungary, 16-17; arrives at Constantinople, 22; makes a treaty with Alexius, 23; besieges Nicaea, 31; fights at Dory-